THE DEVELOPMENT OF
AMERICAN SOCIAL COMEDY
FROM 1787 TO 1936

THE DEVELOPMENT OF AMERICAN SOCIAL COMEDY FROM 1787 TO 1936

———

JOHN GEOFFREY HARTMAN

1971

OCTAGON BOOKS

New York

Reprinted 1971
by special arrangement with the University of Pennsylvania Press

OCTAGON BOOKS
A DIVISION OF FARRAR, STRAUS & GIROUX, INC.
19 Union Square West
New York, N. Y. 10003

LIBRARY OF CONGRESS CATALOG CARD NUMBER: 76-120627

ISBN 0-374-93708-7

Printed in U.S.A. by
NOBLE OFFSET PRINTERS, INC.
NEW YORK 3, N. Y.

Acknowledgment

This volume was written under the direction of Dr. Arthur Hobson Quinn, to whom I am much indebted for his constructive criticism and for his help in locating material. I should also like to thank Mr. Gilbert Emery of Hollywood, California, for sending to me the manuscript of his play *Episode,* and Miss Virginia Gerson and Mr. Otis Skinner of New York City, who gave me information concerning Clyde Fitch and the period in which he achieved his fame. To the many other people who assisted me in the search for material, I wish to express my appreciation.

CONTENTS

CHAPTER I

INTRODUCTION

Social comedy, or the comedy of manners, because of its strict limitations and requirements, appears in America less frequently than any other form of drama. With the slightest over-emphasis upon situation the playwright may immediately descend into farce or melodrama, or should he present his idea just a little too seriously he enters the field of the problem play. Social comedy must always maintain a sense of social values or standards which, according to the treatment of the playwright, either accelerate or retard the action. Frequently it seeks to satirize some particular social craze of the moment, or to reveal for our amusement the embarrassment individuals suffer because of the very conventions and institutions which they themselves have built up and supported. Probably no other form of American drama has suffered more adverse criticism than that of social comedy. All too frequently do we read that, except for a few isolated cases, the comedy of manners has no place in American drama, while there exist, even today, people who will make the blind and sweeping statement that there is no social comedy in America at all! Such a statement comes, of course, from those individuals who feel ashamed that they were born in America and who still cling to the ridiculous fashion of idolizing European culture. It is amazing that this vogue, so old and frayed, still has so strong a hold. To be sure, true social comedy is the last form of drama to develop in any country, for there must be an established society with well developed and sharply defined social codes, a form of society which cannot exist until the material basis for wealth has been built and a class inheriting wealth has been established. At a very early date we find this to have been the case in America, so that it is all the more surprising to hear that not only is this country devoid of social comedy but of cultured society as well.

The chief reason for this mistaken belief lies in the fact that in comparison with European countries the United States is a very new one. When the early settlers came here they had no thought of or time for anything save self preservation, with the result that they banded together regardless of class distinction to protect themselves. Consequently, a far more democratic spirit grew up in America than that which prevailed in England and, to a large extent, has remained ever since. Of course, there were those who attained greater wealth than others and consequently enjoyed privileges denied to the masses, but there is in America a far greater possibility of rising from obscurity to distinction than exists in a country where there is a titled patrician class based upon long established privilege. This in itself instantly presents the American playwright with a difficulty that he must overcome in the opening lines of his play. We cannot tell from reading our program with what element in society the play is going to deal but must wait until the play has begun, so that consequently the American playwright must overcome this obstacle at once. "A British or French playwright can, by the very titles of his dramatis personae prepare the audience for the atmosphere they are to expect. An American playwright must establish the social quality of his characters by their language and actions in the first few moments of the play. This is not an easy task, and his effect may be more easily ruined by a miscasting of parts than in any other form of drama. When all the handicaps are remembered, it is to be wondered, not that we have had so few, but that we have had the sterling examples we possess."[1]

Social comedy reflects the manners of the period with which it deals and is one of the most accurate media we possess for determining the life of that period. Consequently, a dramatist with the necessary qualifications for depicting the social life of his day can portray for posterity the superficial touches and little affectations that change with each generation but which stamp each generation with a definite individuality. Of course, social comedy is not chiefly concerned with presenting superficialities which are simply incidental, but it generally deals with some

---

[1] Quinn, *A History of the American Drama from the Civil War to the Present Day.* Vol. II, p. 85.

question or problem that is of interest at a certain time. Although the novel provides a broader scope, and owing to the fact that it has no set limit to its length, can present a more thorough description and study of the underlying forces with which it deals, nevertheless the drama can portray an age more vividly because of its very living nature. We see the characters alive before us and hear their conversation. A third invaluable source of knowledge for the social historian is correspondence, for here there is an intimate, unstudied tone which reveals exactly the attitude of the writer toward his age or her age. But here, just as in the novel, we miss the real and lifelike representation that the drama alone can give us. Consequently, this study of the comedy of manners in America is one of those preliminary efforts to provide material for the future social historian. There are many descriptions of certain periods in our history, numerous sketches of society, but we lack a full and consecutive history of American manners. It is therefore hoped that this survey may afford a basis for future study.

American social comedy is in most instances an excellent picture of social life as it has changed throughout the different periods. The early plays reflect the manners and customs of the early years of the republic with all the strict conventions that prevailed, while as we progress through the nineteenth century we are aware of the gradual breaking down of many of these conventions and finally of a change in the very fundamental laws of society. We see the complete change in the attitude of children toward their parents taking place from the early days when a father's word was law, to the time when the modern generation swept away all idea of parental authority. We see the evolution of woman from an abject creature to one who holds an equal position with man. This not only pertains to her managing her unmarried life and choosing either a husband or a career, or both, but it reaches out to include the wholly different attitude regarding divorce which exists today from that which prevailed a century ago. To obtain an unbroken picture of the changes of this kind that have taken place in society it is necessary to make a study of the phases of social comedy in America, that is, to take up a certain subject like divorce and trace it from an early date to the present day, rather than to make a study of each playwright in chronological order. But before attacking these phases it is also necessary to trace the progress of American social comedy itself, which for the sake of clarity, we shall divide into five periods.

The first is the Period of Caricature which began with Royall Tyler's *Contrast* in 1787 and continued until about 1860 when, under the influence of Augustin Daly, a change toward a more realistic presentation of life took place. This second period, which includes the work of Bronson Howard, Henry C. deMille, David Belasco, William Gillette and William Dean Howells, we shall call the Transition Period, for it prepared the way for the work of Clyde Fitch which began during the last decade of the nineteenth century. With the plays of Fitch, American social comedy came into its own and this period may well be termed the Establishment of Social Comedy. The next period, the New Century until 1920, includes the work of Augustus Thomas, Langdon Mitchell, Jesse Lynch Williams and Clare Kummer. After 1920 we have the period of Post-War Comedy embracing the work of Philip Barry, Rachel Crothers, Gilbert Emery, S. N. Behrman and others. Since a line obviously must be drawn somewhere, it has seemed best for present purposes not to take up a study of dramatists whose work begins after 1925.

A. THE PERIOD OF CARICATURE

The period of caricature we may say opened officially with "The Contrast," by Royall Tyler, in 1787, for it was the first native comedy acted professionally on our stage. However, two years before, a play entitled *Sans Souci,* alias *Free and Easy: or an Evening's Peep into a Polite Circle,* which was advertised as "An Entire New Entertainment in Three Acts," satirized a certain card game, Sans Souci, which, judging from the conversation in the play, had taken Boston, the "Metropolis of Massachusetts," by storm. The play has no real plot, but is a series of scenes in which several characters, through their conversation, give us a good picture of what amusements were in vogue in society and of the opposing views held by the old school and the rebellious younger people. It all seems very similar to modern times. In the closing scene there is some fairly crisp dialogue between four card players which lifts the play out of the category of a series of dissertations. There is no evidence that the play was acted, nor is the author known, although it has been attributed to Mrs. Mercy Warren who wrote some Revolutionary satires, the best known of which is probably *The Group*.[2]

In one conversation between Madame Importance and Madame Brilliant, there is every evidence that social lines were distinctly marked, for the former fears that the women dress too lavishly at the card parties, to which the latter replies:

> "Don't be apprehensive on this account—this is the very thing I was in hopes would take place—this will serve to *sift down families* and will be the most effectual means to establish a *precedency*."

The Contrast, produced in 1787, contains two caricatures, that of Jonathan, the New England Yankee, and that of Dimple, the good-for-nothing rake of his day who fashions his ways after the teachings of Lord Chesterfield. Jonathan became the prototype of one of the most famous characters on the American stage, for the popularity of the Yankee held the boards far into the nineteenth century. Characters like Dimple seem to have served the purpose of contrast between affected young men with no principles and the hero who was always pure gold. We find them still abounding in the plays during the fifties. These dandies of the early days were apparently garbed in the most elaborate fashion. The costume consisted of a 'red coat, single breasted, long waisted, pocket flaps, high-cut standing collar trimmed with gold lace; satin knee breeches with knee buckles (silver or paste); silk stockings with fancy clocks; pumps with set silver buckles; heels of shoes red, stitched with silk; sometimes two watches with trinkets dependent, as chains from the fobs on either side of the small clothes; three-cornered cocked hat, looped up in front with gold loop and button, hair powdered and clubbed behind; ruffled bosoms to shirt, hand

---

[2] Quinn, *A History of the American Drama from the Beginning to the Civil War,* p. 63

ruffles of lace, gold-headed cane and tassel, buttons of coat gold
tissue, size of half dollar![3]   The ball room dress was far more
elaborate, and to men of the present time who are caught in the
turmoil of a complicated civilization, would serve as an excuse
for never attending a formal function or would drive them to
suicide.   A dandy was called a "Macaroni," a term used by
Sheridan in his *School for Scandal.*

In connection with these two characters it might be wise to
consider several others for the benefit of those people who need-
lessly lament the absence of any social life in this country.   To
begin with, we have Colonel Manly and his sister Charlotte, who
obviously hold an assured social position.   The very fact that
Manly is a colonel establishes him at once as a gentleman, for to
be an officer implied unquestioned social standing.   Charlotte, his
sister, is a girl whose right to social leadership is owing not only
to her attractive personality, but also to the apparent fact that
she is a gentlewoman accustomed to an atmosphere of refinement.
Her friend, Letitia, is a girl like her and from their gossip we can
form a good opinion of the fashionable life of their day.   The
girls are vivacious and gay in sharp contrast to Colonel Manly
who is a rather solemn individual.   He represents the finest ideals
in an American and is the direct opposite of Dimple, the affected
rake.   The social scene which forms the background of the play
could hardly exist if there had been no social life.   In regard to
this particular matter let us survey briefly some of the social
phases in early American life.

New England, to be sure, boasted of being very democratic but
in reality was oligarchic.   The very fact that the Eighteenth
Century New Englanders tried to avoid contrasts and conflicts in
order to preserve an atmosphere of serenity, proves that they
recognized the differences which are bound to exist between the
classes that compose society as a whole.   Despite the stress they
laid upon education, religion and the serious side of life, and their
attempt to appear democratic, the term "Tory Row" in Cambridge
signifies that there was a group of wealthy, prominent families

---

[3] Durang, *History of the Philadelphia Stage between the Years 1749 and
1855,* Vol. I, p. 22.

who were proud of their position and clung to it. We may be reasonably sure that they did not live in a pinched style, but surrounded themselves with every comfort. Certainly, in the next century, Mrs. Basil Hall who, with her husband, made a fourteen month sojourn through America, 1827-1828, found society in Boston more to her liking than that which she encountered elsewhere, largely because of the quiet elegance with which she was entertained. In a letter to her sister in which she describes a dinner party at Professor Ticknor's she says, "All was well ordered and the style particularly handsome."[4]

Whatever Mrs. Hall may have thought of Boston society in the eighteen twenties, Philadelphia was the social center during the first decades of the Republic just as it had been in Colonial days, for it led both in the development of the theatre and of music and was, besides, the intellectual center of the country. The Quakers, of course, were opposed to both music and the theatre but they did not practice the severe measures of suppression that we find in New England. On the other hand, the Episcopal Church element was favorable to artistic development and under this group there grew up an interest in both music and the theatre.

Among many of the delightful social functions that took place were gatherings of music lovers at the homes of Francis Hopkinson, John Penn and Dr. Kuhn. Hopkinson, an accomplished musician, was untiring in his efforts to promote this art and was one of the guiding lights prior to the American Revolution in the development of concert life in Philadelphia. For, despite many private musical functions, we find that "public and half-public concerts remained comparatively few before the war."[5] Aided by Giovanni Gualdo, an Italian wine merchant, and James Bremner, Hopkinson seems to have finally broken down the barriers that had obstructed the path to musical development. It was during these days that church music showed marked improvement while music was introduced at Commencement and an Orpheus Club was formed.

---

[4] *The Aristocratic Journey.* Edited by Una Pope-Hennessy, p. 88.
[5] Sonneck, *Early Concert Life in America,* p. 66.

The City Fathers of Boston apparently did not have the same objections to music that they had to the theatre, for as early as 1731 concerts were advertised and there is reason to believe that they had been going on long before this date. Furthermore, a Peter Pelham, who promoted musical activity in Boston and taught dancing, also filled the capacity of manager of the subscription assembly which confirms the assertion that there was an exclusive social group in New England. Salem, always noted for its witch-burning, seems to have indulged in a more agreeable pastime by 1739, for we read that Charles Bradstreet obtained permission from the selectmen to "teach dancing" in connection with French "so long as he keeps good order."[6] Similarly, a little later, a Frenchman, Lawrence D'Obleville, taught dancing and good manners to the children and youth of Salem and other towns.

Probably the most interesting musical organization in this country was the Saint Cecilia Society of Charleston, South Carolina, which was founded in 1737 and continued to furnish excellent concerts until the latter part of the nineteenth century when it became merely an "exclusive assembly for exclusive society."[7] Concerts were given every two weeks and musicians were advertised for as far away as Boston. The rules of the society were many and seem to have omitted nothing which goes to make an organization. South Carolina, with Charleston as its center, seems to have enjoyed a more worldly social life than any other city during Colonial days—at least a more unrestricted social life —for there were neither New England Puritans nor Philadelphia Quakers to scowl upon amusements. In one account of the early days in this state we are informed that the planters of South Carolina were "the wealthiest, the most travelled and least provincial of the Southern slave owners."[8] South Carolina was "more in touch with England than other Southern colonies, while in the matter of social and educational amenities Charleston was noted as being almost the rival of Boston and Philadelphia, with characteristics of its own superadded."[9] Theatrical life flourished

---

[6] Wharton, *Colonial Days and Dames,* p. 54.
[7] Sonneck, *Early Concert Life in America,* p. 16.
[8] Bradley, *Colonial Americans in Exile,* p. 35.
[9] *Ibid.,* p. 34.

there, English actors as well as local talent playing before enthusiastic audiences. Wealthy Southern planters who could afford leisure came to Charleston for the season and all in all it seems to have been a gay and colorful center.

This planter aristocracy of the South seems to have been rivalled in Colonial times by the Patroon system which flourished along the banks of the Hudson River in New York State. At the time of the founding of Albany "A gentleman of the name of Rensselaer was considered as in a manner lord paramount of this city, a preeminence which his successor still enjoys, both with regard to the town and lands adjacent. The original proprietor obtained from the High and Mighty States a grant of lands, which, from the church, extended twelve miles in every direction, forming a manor twenty-four Dutch miles in length, and the same in breadth, including lands not only of the best quality of any in the province, but the most happily situated for the purposes both of commerce and of agriculture." The proprietor was looked up to as much as "republicans in a new country" could look up to anyone. "He was called the Patroon, a designation tantamount to lord of the manor." However, his powers were limited for none of the lands could be either sold or alienated, and the leases held good "while water runs and grass grows." The landlord received a tenth sheaf of every kind of grain that the ground produced, but otherwise he could make no demands so that those who held leases under him actually had all the independence of proprietors without the pride of property. Families who took extensive leases from the Patroon were the Cuylers, Schuylers, Philipses and Cortlandts.[10]

New York City was the center for these wealthy families in the winter where they enjoyed a great diversity of amusements, while in the summer they ensconced themselves on their estates along the Hudson or on Long Island. A brilliant social life seems to have been enjoyed on these estates, for here as in the South, there was an air of freedom.

As we have already seen, a post-war gaiety broke forth in

---

[10] Grant, *Memoirs of an American Lady*, pp. 18-19.

Boston after the American Revolution. In New York, where a comparatively lively time had continued during the conflict largely because of the presence of British officers, there was not the same contrast in the mode of life after the Revolution. In Philadelphia, however, where theatres had been closed except during the British occupation, and in fact where any unnecessary and frivolous amusement which entailed the spending of money had been banned, the years following the close of hostilities brought a new sparkle to life. During this period when Philadelphia was the capital of the new republic there was a burst of social gaiety never before known there, for naturally it was the center for what always seems to be known as the "diplomatic set" and this in itself invariably holds a certain fascination for society. Here, indeed, many belles who have since figured in American history of that period reigned in all their glory.

When Washington was finally chosen as the permanent site for the national capital, Philadelphia still was the social center for these people because for many years Washington remained a primitive country village. The wives of our statesmen seem to have been more than reluctant to isolate themselves in Washington, and so we find them spending their time in Philadelphia, either visiting friends or relatives for the season, or actually living there in houses secured by their husbands. There is a certain charm about that period which never again seems to have marked any age in the history of America.

In the light of this early social life it seems a pity that there were not more comedies of manners but, with a few exceptions, the comedies until around 1860 were social *satires* for they were filled with sharp jibes and a boldly plain humor that was meant to devastate the object of ridicule. Certain types of people and popular fads were held up as objects of derision, the exaggerated treatment of them lasting until about 1860, when Augustin Daly dominated the American stage and began drawing characters in a more true and real light.

Also, during the period of caricature there flourished a French vogue which had its beginning just after the Revolution when a hostile attitude toward England prevailed. *The Contrast* shows this earlier ill feeling, for Tyler ridicules the affectations of the Anglomaniac, contrasting the people who adopted these affectations with the sound Americans. However, the French vogue finally went so far that in the social comedies which center around the middle of the nineteenth century we find dramatists poking fun at the socially ambitious wives who ape French manners, Mrs. Tiffany in *Fashion* (1845) being the most famous. Another of these characters is Mrs. Apex in the play *Self* (1856), but besides Mrs. Tiffany she fades into comparative insignificance. The French Revolution won widespread sympathy in this country, coming as it did immediately after the American Revolution and as usual people's feelings ran away with them. Everything had to be French. James Nelson Barker in his *Tears and Smiles* (1808) presents us with the character, Fluttermore, an affected young man who feels that one must have French ways to be really worth anything; he can stand neither America nor Americans.

The American Academy of Arts and Sciences in New England tried to reproduce "the air of France rather than of England and to follow the Academy rather than the Royal Society."[11] Similarly, in Virginia, a French officer, supported by the lieutenant governor of the commonwealth, started an Academy of Arts and Sciences and obtained subscriptions, but the French Revolution proved a stumbling block in the matter of funds.

Poems and plays appeared which dealt with various phases and incidents of the French Revolution but it was not until William Dunlap's untiring efforts in the field of adaptation that French plays became popular. The introduction of the melodrama in 1803 gave real impetus to interest in French drama.[12] Following Dunlap's activity came the numerous adaptations of John Howard Payne, whose finest comedy, *Charles the Second* (1824) is an adaptation of *La Jeunesse de Henri V* by Alexandre Duval, which in turn was based on *Charles II, roi d'Angleterre, en un certain lieu,* by Sébastien Mercier. The play, *Charles the Second,* is romantic with the tone and spirit of high comedy, and is one

---

[11] Beard, *The Rise of American Civilization,* part I, p. 442.
[12] Schoenberger, *American Adaptations of French Plays on the New York and Philadelphia Stages from 1790-1833,* p. 8.

which we shall take up for further discussion when considering
this particular genre.

The third outstanding playwright of this period whose adaptations from the French were popular on the American stage was
Richard Penn Smith. The popularity of the melodrama continued until the end of this early period although at the same time
the *original* work of American playwrights generally did not
follow this trend. The romantic wave which had swept the
Continent had reached our shores, and this ultimately gave way
to realistic comedies about the middle of the century. Thus there
were two separate trends in the drama here, the adaptations of
French melodrama and the original romantic and realistic plays.[13]

As already stated, the comedies of the early period were generally
satiric and it will be seen readily that they dealt with the parvenu
rather than with people whose position in society was assured.
The first comedies, notably *The Contrast,* do not fall into this
category but those of the middle nineteenth century nearly always
portrayed socially ambitious people. *Fashion* (1845), *Self* (1856),
and *The Golden Calf* (1857) all center around the parvenu.
Wheat and Chaff (1858) by D. W. Wainwright and W. H.
Hurlburt's *Americans in Paris* (1858) are exceptions, although
the former contains some characters of this type. However, the
very fact that the playwrights so frequently show individuals who
were attempting to force their way into circles for which they
were not qualified proves that there was an element composed of
gentlemen and gentlewomen.

Frederika Bremer, the Swedish novelist, who made a tour of
this country in 1849 and 1850, published the letters she had written
to her sister in Sweden. The two volume work, entitled *The
Homes of the New World : Impressions of America,* gives a very
intimate and accurate picture of life during the middle of the
nineteenth century. Miss Bremer's first impressions of America
were received in New York for she went to the Astor House
immediately upon her arrival. "The Astor House and its splendid
rooms, and social life and the 'New World' steamer, with all its

---

[13] Ware, *American Adaptations of French Plays on the New York and
Philadelphia Stages from 1834 to the Civil War,* p. 10.

finery, were good specimens of the showy side of the life of the New World."[14] However, she stayed in New York but a short time for a Mr. and Mrs. Downing entertained her in their home along the Hudson where she evidently enjoyed a charming social life. Her descriptions of her visit with these people and of the warm hospitality extended to her wherever she went in this country reveal the existence of a side of life which so rarely appeared in the drama during this period.

Added to this are the accounts of the social life of the nineteenth century in Virginia Tatnall Peacock's *Famous American Belles of the Nineteenth Century.* Among the many well known women who appear in this book is Octavia Walton, later Madame Le Vert. Octavia Walton was the granddaughter of George Walton, one of the signers of the Declaration of Independence, at one time governor of Georgia and later a member of the Supreme Court. Not only was Octavia a woman of high intellectual attainment but she was a true cosmopolite who made lasting friendships with some of the foremost figures of that period. She corresponded with Washington Irving and aroused the admiration of Henry Clay by her brilliant conversation. When traveling on the Continent she spoke with equal ease Italian, French and Spanish. Among Madame Le Vert's distinguished guests in her home in Mobile, Alabama, were Frederika Bremer, Kossuth and Lady Emmeline Stuart Wortley, daughter of the Duke of Rutland.[15] Lady Wortley later gave Madame Le Vert an introduction in England which made possible her social fame there. One of the many honors accorded to the American woman was an invitation to a court ball before she had been presented to the Queen.[16]

Another account which describes a very delightful social element in America appears in the *Americana* for 1936, Vol. 30, third quarter. The author of this article, Margaret Lente Raoul, has given us a picture of the group which centered around Gouverneur Kemble whom General Winfield Scott called the "most perfect gentleman in the United States."

[14] Bremer, *The Homes of the New World,* Vol. I, p. 19.
[15] Peacock, *Famous American Belles of the Nineteenth Century,* p. 102.
[16] *Ibid,* pp. 111 and 113.

Among Gouverneur Kemble's friends were Washington Irving, William Cullen Bryant, Hugh Legaré, President Van Buren and Robert E. Lee. Kemble's residence was at Cold Spring, New York, where the main shop of the West Point Foundry, of which he was head, was located. He inherited Mt. Pleasant on the Passaic, near Newark, and there he with Irving and Paulding began the *Salmagundi Papers*. The social life of Kemble's group is described as being "more catholic, more cosmopolitan, more cultivated than that pictured in Edith Wharton's 'A Backward Glance'. " It was an honor indeed to be invited to the famous Saturday dinners at Cold Spring. The guests were all men since in those days women were not supposed to be actively interested in art and literature. Kemble possessed the second finest collection of paintings in America so that artists as well as writers gathered at his house. Among his friends from abroad were Prince Louis Napoleon, Lord Hartington, later Duke of Devonshire, and Fanny Kemble, the famous English actress.

One is constantly running across scattered accounts of charming social life in America but this phase of life did not figure largely in literature, particularly in the drama, and except for the very early years of the Republic true social comedy is conspicuous chiefly for its rarity. At first glance it may seem strange that the very early comedies were more truly comedies of manners than those which came during the latter part of this period of caricature, but when one reviews American history the fact becomes obvious. In the early days of the United States there was a well established and very distinct society, one into which it was far more difficult to force one's way than it was later when the wheels of industry began to revolutionize the country and to cause one vast upheaval after another.

There are several reasons which may account for the lack of social comedy during the latter part of this period. In the first place, from a literary standpoint, it was as we have seen, the romantic age. Plays like Robert Montgomery Bird's *Gladiator* (1831), and *The Broker of Bogota* (1834), and Nathaniel Parker Willis' *Tortesa the Usurer* (1839), held the spotlight on the stage. We have also pointed out the interest in melodrama.

In the second place, already noted, it was an age of great expansion and one in which politics absorbed people's interest to a great extent. The excitement over Andrew Jackson's campaign and the results of his administration held public attention for many years. In connection with Jackson we find what was probably a third reason why social comedy had so little appeal—the rise of the "common man." Great emphasis fell upon this individual, for the age was one when a man was judged particularly by what he could *do,* not by what he thought, or what he was, or what his family had been, but upon his ability to accomplish a great deal in a short time. Thus during a period when stress was laid upon the working man, social comedy very likely did not have wide popular appeal.

One fact which is undeniable is that during the decades immediately preceding the Civil War, America was progressing at an astonishing pace in all walks of life. There were then, just as there were during the nineteen twenties, numberless new-rich families who were struggling for a place in the sun. Perhaps this spectacle with the amusing aspects which naturally accompany it caught the fancy of the dramatist and appealed to the public. At any rate, the plays of the forties and fifties centered around this theme.

B.   THE TRANSITION PERIOD

After the Civil War, America witnessed great changes in the social order. This disturbance of social standards arose not only from the destruction of established fortunes in both the North and the South, but also from the acquisition of great fortunes in many cases by those who had not enjoyed them before. In the South there was a more permanent aristocracy since it was based upon land holding: and although the Southerners lost their fortunes and were practically destitute for many years after the war, in many instances they still retained their land. These old families were held indissolubly together not only by their unconquerable pride but by their intense bitterness against the North. In the history of American social comedy very few scenes have been laid in the South. While social life in Southern cities such as

Charleston was charming and cultured to a high degree before the Civil War, nevertheless the greater part of Southern social life centered around the large plantations. Social comedy seems to thrive best in cities. The stir and bustle and competition of a metropolis, along with the complex problems of urban life, seem to add verve and zest and brilliancy to conversation.

It was in the North that the great readjustment in society took place. Many families whose position and wealth depended largely upon commerce lost everything when this failed them. However, to counter-balance this loss of wealth on the part of some of the older, well established families, new channels opened through which vast fortunes were built by many people who were formerly obscure. For it was during this period that rail communication between the Atlantic and Pacific coasts was completed, and this made possible the development of the great resources of our country. Tremendous wealth was amassed through the opening of coal and oil fields in Pennsylvania and West Virginia while in the Far West the mining of gold and silver brought undreamed of riches to many. This was the age when lumber barons, oil magnates, railroad kings and great manufacturers dominated the world of finance and politics with no interference from the former slave owning aristocracy of the South.

Great cities grew up throughout the West. Not content to be leaders in the parts of the country in which they had amassed their wealth the socially ambitious flocked to the cities along the Atlantic seaboard. New York, especially, became their mecca. Their ambition was to have the old New York families accept them socially. When they found this more difficult than they had anticipated they resorted to every means of expenditure in their mode of living and in their style of entertainment. Gradually, they contracted marriages with families of the old order who had become impoverished. By the end of the century "the masters of great urban wealth dominated the social plain."[17]

However, very little of this readjustment seems to have appeared in the drama until the time of Clyde Fitch. Whether the

---

[17] Beard, *The Rise of American Civilization*, Vol. II, p. 383.

older established group maintained its position longer than is generally supposed or whether, as is so often the case, a change like the one that took place in the seventies and eighties, was more noticeable in retrospect is a matter of conjecture. Unlike the comedies of the forties and fifties, those of the transition period do not deal with the parvenu nor do they contrast the self-made man with the older established families. William Dean Howells deals with these characters in some of his novels, the most notable being *The Rise of Silas Lapham,* but his plays do not reflect them.

Bronson Howard is the American dramatist of this period to whom we must turn for social comedies which reflect contemporary life. Gillette, Herne and Harrigan who wrote at the same time, were interested in developing other phases of drama, while the attempts of Edgar Fawcett and Olive Logan in the field of social comedy were anything but happy. Had they been competent dramatists one cannot help but feel that they would have been successful, for Howard's popularity proves that the public enjoyed drama that recognized social values. However, unlike Howells' comedies, Howard's dealt with definite social problems caused by the increasing complexity of life. Howells' one act plays were either farces or pure comedies of manners and perhaps managers felt that they lacked sufficient conflict to attract a following. They saw, too, that there was no market for the one act play except in vaudeville. At any rate, managers failed to produce them in America, but in England two of these plays met instant popularity. Whatever may be the reason for the drama not reflecting the social readjustments that took place during these decades, the transition period marked an important change in our society.

The work of Augustin Daly marked a new era in American drama, for while many of his characters are types, nevertheless they are not exaggerated to the point of caricature as are so many of the characters in the forties and fifties. Nor did Daly wield the weapon of satire with the same sharp invective as his predecessors. He is more subtle, presents his characters in a more natural way, while the dialogue is less stilted and at times reaches a high order of bright repartee. The note of true social comedy is frequently struck in his plays. Chiefly remarkable for his excellent adaptations from both the French and German drama, two of Daly's native plays *Divorce* and *Pique*, were in the field of social comedy. Since the former belongs to a definite phase of American social comedy we shall consider it at another time.

Pique, produced at the New Fifth Avenue Theatre, December 14th, 1875, while chiefly a domestic comedy, preserves the atmosphere and standards of the comedy of manners, contrasting very well the straightforward New England honesty and strict principles with an unethical urban group of New Yorkers. The scenes are laid in "Grassmere," a country seat on the Hudson, and in Old Deerfield, New England. The plot deals with a woman who out of pique has accepted the hand of a man whom she does not love, because the one whom she thinks she loves, has proposed to her young step-mother on account of her money. The girl cannot at first adjust herself to her husband's New England principles nor will she try to get along with his family. Finally, after she realizes the worthless character of her former lover she learns to love her husband. The play passes into melodrama at one point, reminding us that this vogue was still popular, but the social laws which govern the actions of the characters, laws which their pride and sense of fitness will not let them break, belong to the comedy of manners.

What is particularly remarkable in Daly's adaptations from the French and German drama is the fact that the versions in English have no foreign flavor whatever. Daly seems to have followed his models closely but to have felt that certain changes were necessary for the sake of clarity. For instance, in *The Lottery of Love* (1889), he has two servants establish the state of affairs that we are to expect. The French play, *Les Suprises du Divorce,* by Alexandre Bisson and Antony Mars, does not have this scene at all, but begins at once with the main action. Of course, Daly Anglicizes the names; Mrs. Sherramy, the fiendish mother-in-law, being Madame Bonivard in the French version. And in connection with this particular character Daly has made an interesting change. Madame Bonivard we discover had been a famous dancer, or at least prided herself upon being a toast of the town, but in the American play we find that she had been a Bloomer girl. Now the Bloomer girls constituted part of the feminist movement which began to make itself audible about the middle of the nineteenth century. It was all part of the general uproar made by the unshrinking pioneers in their fight for women's rights and this particular phase began when in 1851, Mrs. Elizabeth Smith Miller, daughter of Congressman Gerrit Smith of New York, surprised the nation's capital by appearing "dressed somewhat in the Turkish style." This unseemly (and one might add unsightly) costume was, above the waist, like any other dress, but the skirt fell just below the knee while underneath it were full, baggy trousers of broadcloth, gathered together at the ankle with an elastic band. Clad in this amazing semi-Turkish attire, Mrs. Miller invaded Seneca Falls, New York, where Mrs. Dexter C. Bloomer, another ardent supporter of various movements—it was temperance at the moment—immediately adopted the new mode of dress. Although the followers of this particular phase in the fight for freedom had to abandon their costume eventually because of untold ridicule, Mrs. Bloomer's name still clings to a certain article of feminine apparel. Under it all there lies not a little pathos, for in the words of Mr. Russel Crouse, "It seems a little curious that with the lady herself gone and forgotten almost any gust of wind can lift a feminine skirt and reveal the only monument she has in a day and age when both prohibition and women's suffrage, her favorite causes, are written into the Constitution."[18] Since the publication of Mr. Crouse's book, prohibition, of course, has given place to repeal, so perhaps it is as well that Mrs. Bloomer has joined the shades.

Madame Bonivard poses for a picture in an old dancing costume, while Mrs. Sherramy, her American counterpart, poses in her old Bloomer costume. A change of this kind on Daly's part shows his cleverness in selecting a native incident which appealed to American audiences. The appearance of Mrs. Sherramy in this garb combined with the sudden transformation of her character from a disagreeable woman to a silly, simpering woman who

[18] Crouse, *Mr. Currier and Mr. Ives,* p. 64.

recalls a wild incident in New Orleans when she was jailed on the
grounds of not being respectable, must have sent the spectators
in the theatre into an uproar. Other than this, there are very few
alterations in the play. One character, Corbulon, uncle of Henri,
in the French play, is simply made an old friend of Doubledot in
the American version, while at the end of the American comedy
one of the characters recites a poem, and the French one ends
with the observations: "Le mariage est une loterie" and "Et le
divorce une boîte a surprises!" One prefers the French ending,
for the little moralizing verses attached to the end of the plays
during this period of our drama seem extremely annoying today.

From *Krieg im Frieden* by Gustav von Moser, Daly made the
adaptation *The Passing Regiment* (1881). The German play is
laid in the home of Heindorf, in a provincial town, while Daly
has for his setting the home of the Winthrops at Narragansett
Pier. Other than a change of names and the fact that the action
is laid in this country instead of in Germany, there seems to be
little difference between the two plays. Daly has followed the
original very closely in this case even in the opening scene where
a servant has just given the morning mail to one of the young
girls in the play. She is interrupted in the reading of a letter from
her husband by her cousin, a Russian girl. The conversation between the two girls is practically identical in both plays. To
translate the social standards of one country to another is more
easily accomplished than to try to interpret either political questions, religious beliefs or business methods. Social standards are
fundamentally the same in different countries and are more lasting than the laws governing public affairs, to say nothing of the
completely different aspects that the latter have in various nations.
There is not the same contemporaneous quality about social laws
that there is about public questions. In Daly's plays the fact that
the social atmosphere does not seem altered is because we are
confronted with people belonging socially to the same class. In
the comedy of manners the same social creeds hold for one country as for another. The particular group of people represented,
except for speaking a different language, recognize the same laws.
A gentleman or gentlewoman of one country needs no introduction
to those of another.

From *Reif von Reiflingen* by von Moser which the author had written as a sequel to *Krieg im Frieden* Daly made the adaptation *Our English Friend,* 1882. This play, however, is not a sequel to *The Passing Regiment,* for an Englishman is the central character and it is important to note that for once he is not caricatured. Almost without exception in American drama prior to Daly, it had been the custom to caricature any character who was not American, so that to find one who is a human being is refreshing. But this play as well as several other of Daly's adaptations we shall discuss in another place.

To the transition period belong also Bronson Howard, William Dean Howells, Henry C. deMille and David Belasco. The work of these men reflects the growing realism both in the manner of writing plays and in the presentation of characters. Belasco, a romanticist, is nevertheless famous for his realistic stage settings, while added to the men just mentioned, one must remember that during these years the quiet, natural acting of William Gillette caused what was almost a revolution in that particular field of expression. All of these forces which tended toward a more realistic representation of life on the stage contributed to the progress of social comedy, for in this particular field there can be no caricature or forced, unnatural modes of expression if the play is to reveal the element in society with which the comedy of manners is concerned.

Until the time of Bronson Howard playwriting as a means of livelihood was a practically hopeless struggle in America. Professional playwrights there had been in William Dunlap, John Howard Payne, Joseph Stevens Jones and Augustin Daly, but these men, besides being playwrights, were also connected with the theatre either as actors, producers or managers. Robert Montgomery Bird and George Henry Boker were more strictly playwrights. The former tried to live by this means but because of too great obstacles had to turn to other fields of writing as well. However, with the appearance of Howard upon the scene a new age dawned for American playwrights because Howard *succeeded* as a professional dramatist. His career from 1870 to 1906 showed a steady development of his own powers and paralleled a steadily growing achievement in the American drama as a whole.

The work of Howard runs side by side with that of Daly but there is evident at the same time a step forward toward a more true social comedy. However, it was largely owing to Daly that the opportunity in the field of social comedy was afforded Howard, for Daly produced his *Saratoga* in 1870 followed by *Diamonds* in 1872. Strictly speaking, *Saratoga* is a farce comedy in which the characters are types and in which the action depends mainly upon situation, but it served at the time to satirize the social craze for the popular resort. Underneath the farcical actions lies a sure sense of social values, but the play on the whole reminds us of the stilted plays of the fifties. It was not until twelve years later that Howard produced his first fine social comedy. With the production of *Young Mrs. Winthrop* in 1882, American audiences witnessed for the first time a true social comedy, always excepting Tyler's *Contrast* in 1787. While we have spoken of the earlier plays as social comedies we have also seen that nearly all of them were satires. Although Augustin Daly passed out of the category of satire, the characters were generally conventional types. *Young Mrs. Winthrop* is a play in which the characters' actions are a result of the forces which govern their lives, of the age in which they live, and what is of still greater importance, there is an immediate recognition on the part of the audience that Constance and Douglas Winthrop are cultured, well-bred people. Howard made no attempt to establish this fact. It is obvious at once. This play and *Kate* (1905), (the latter published in a form halfway between the novel and the drama), are Howard's two finest social comedies, for in both there is no perceptible effort to establish an atmosphere of refinement. It seems to arise out of the very nature of the characters.

Henry C. deMille and David Belasco collaborated in writing several plays, two which, *Lord Chumley* and *The Charity Ball,* while tending toward romance, preserve the atmosphere and tone of social comedy. The former has an English setting and deals with English characters exclusively, while the latter is laid in New York. In both of these plays there is a great deal of sentiment which at times becomes a little hard to swallow, while a definite tendency to draw a moral is obvious. The romantic vein in the work of deMille and Belasco is very likely owing to the latter, for in *John Delmer's Daughters,* written solely by deMille, there is less of it, the play reflecting contemporary life in a more realistic manner.

When we turn to the work of William Dean Howells we can ask for nothing more in the depiction of actual human beings with all their little foolish fancies and their slavish adherence to convention. Although the majority of Howells' one act plays were farces, we cannot forget many of the characters, the sparkling dialogue and the complete understanding of values they reveal. Three of these plays rise above farce to the level of social comedy. They do not depend purely upon situation for their effect but upon the laws that govern human action under certain circumstances, the social creeds that form the basis of society. Whether one has seen or simply read these plays he will never forget the brilliant dialogue, the characterization, and the astounding ease with which Howells has created the whole picture.

Five O'Clock Tea (1889), which opens with Mrs. Amy Somers parading before her mirror to see whether her dress billows in a graceful manner while Willis Campbell is watching, unknown to her, contains repartee of a brilliance rare in literature. At the same time, the play is a masterpiece in revealing the deeper feelings that lie beneath our conventional behavior and light, superficial conversation. Willis Campbell has proposed to Mrs. Somers (who is a widow and who will accept him when she has tortured him sufficiently) before any of her tea guests have arrived. After Mr. Bemis, an elderly gentleman, has come, they are discussing tea with lemon, which Mrs. Somers dislikes.

> Campbell: "Well, I can think of something much worse than tea with lemon in it."
> Mrs. Somers: "What?"
> Campbell: "No tea at all."
> Mrs. Somers, recollecting herself: "Oh, *poor* Mr. Campbell! Two lumps?"
> Campbell: "One, thank you. Your pity is so sweet!"
> Mrs. Somers: "You ought to have thought of the milk of human kindness, and spared my cream-jug too."

> Campbell: "You didn't pour out your compassion soon
> enough."
> Bemis, who has been sipping his tea in silent admiration:
> "Are you often able to keep it up in that way? I
> was fancying myself at the theatre."
> Mrs. Somers: "Oh, don't encore us. Mr. Campbell
> would keep saying his things over indefinitely."
> Campbell, presenting his cup: "Another lump. It's
> turned bitter. *Two!*"

The double meaning in each remark is, of course, obvious, for
Mrs. Somers has just rejected Campbell's proposal a few minutes
earlier.

Another telling bit of dialogue and a scene which shows how
delightfully Howells ridicules our social manners arises when Mrs.
Curwen arrives.

> Mrs. Somers: "Oh, there is Mrs. Curwen!" (To Camp-
> bell, aside) "And without her husband!"
> Campbell: "Or anyone else's husband."
> Mrs. Somers: "For shame!"
> Campbell: "You began it."
> Mrs. Somers, to Mrs. Curwen, who approaches her sofa:
> "You are kindness itself, Mrs. Curwen, to come on
> such a day." The ladies press each other's hands.
> Mrs. Curwen: "You are goodness in person, Mrs. Som-
> ers, to say so."
> Campbell: "And I am magnanimity embodied. Let me
> introduce myself, Mrs. Curwen!" He bows, and
> Mrs. Cuwen deeply curtsies.
> Mrs. Curwen: "I should never have known you."
> Campbell, melodramatically, to Mrs. Somers: "Tea,
> ho! for Mrs. Curwen—impenetrably disguised as
> kindness."

The play is an excellent illustration of one of the phases of
social comedy which we shall discuss later.

A Likely Story (1889) is nearer farce, but the opening scene
in which Amy Campbell (who was Mrs. Somers in *Five O'Clock
Tea*) reads notes of acceptance and regret in reply to her invita-
tions to a garden party, reaches the level of social comedy. The
various replies, such as, "The Morgans are 'sorrow stricken,'"

"Mrs. Stevenson is 'bowed to the earth,'" "Colonel Murphree is 'overjoyed,'" give us choice examples of the exaggerated, polite phraseology in which people revelled. The dialogue between Willis and Amy Campbell is sparkling and almost incredibly real.

With *The Unexpected Guests* in 1893, Howells attained the peak of perfection in the comedy of manners. The play is a priceless example of magnificent technique in polite lying—or perhaps one should say in revealing to what extremities the social laws force us under trying circumstances. Mr. and Mrs. Belfort, whom Mrs. Campbell *thinks* have declined her dinner invitation, arrive, just as the assembled guests are ready to dine. Far, far better to die than to tell them the ghastly predicament into which she is plunged, insists Amy Campbell to her husband. Everyone except the Belforts finally becomes aware of the situation, until even they discover the dilemma when a loud voice echoes from the hall telephoning to the club for more quail. Instead of being overcome, however, Amy Campbell rises to the occasion and is even more charming, if possible, when she reveals the truth and admits that she didn't expect the Belforts and before everyone reads the note of acceptance which she thought one of regret. By the simple act of making a clean breast of everything in the beginning no confusion or agony of mind could have arisen, but to be honest under the circumstances would, to Amy, have been a breach of etiquette totally unforgivable. The play is pure social comedy, based as it is upon a purely artificial convention, and yet one which at the moment calls forth every possible resource at hand. Howells thoroughly enjoys displaying the misery we suffer owing to social codes and yet, in the end, shows the triumph of good breeding when we can *gracefully* take the bull by the horns. One of the most delightful touches of all in this play is the phonograph which at each prevarication chants "Truth crushed to earth shall rise again." Almost no other part of the recording can be heard for the phonograph was still in a state of imperfection. The use of the invention is typical of Howells' realism and his keeping abreast of the times.

Some of his other one act plays which are more nearly farce but which still maintain the tone and atmosphere of social comedy because of their preservation of the fundamental laws of society are *A Previous Engagement, An Indian Giver, The Mouse Trap, Evening Dress* and *The Elevator*. In the last mentioned we are confronted by a distraught hostess—for only half of her dinner guests have arrived. What has happened is that the others are stuck half way between the fourth and fifth floors in an elevator, another invention which obviously was far from perfection. The conversation between those caught in mid-air and those who are in the apartment who try to offer suggestions (all of them ridiculous) and comforting remarks is, for a revelation of human nature under trying conditions, incomparable. The utterly inane "Don't move" from above, and the reply "We're stone" from the depths, and "How long have you been there?" with the answer "Since the world began" illustrate the state into which everyone is plunged. And yet, in spite of the fact that the *situation* is really the basis of the play, the characters and dialogue rise so far above farce that the play is on the borderline of the comedy of manners.

In *Evening Dress* we again have a farcical situation, but before this scene takes place we discover Mr. and Mrs. Roberts in one of those marital discussions that inevitably occur before an evening's entertainment. Mr. Roberts has returned from a trip completely exhausted, but must go to a musicale. Too tired to protest, he is listening to his wife's endless instructions which are interspersed with words of commiseration of his condition.

> Agnes Roberts: "You *are* dreadfully used up, Edward, and I think it's cruel to make you go out; but what can I do? If it was anybody but Mrs. Miller I wouldn't think of having you go; I'm sure I never want to have her about, anyway. But that's just the kind of people that you're a perfect slave to!" . . .
>
> Mrs. Campbell (who has arrived to take Mrs. Roberts to the musicale): "The worst of a bore like her is that she's sure to come to all *your* things, and you can't get off from one of hers." . . .

Edward Roberts misses the affair owing to Agnes' forgetting to tell him where his dress suit is. When the ladies return home a scene of wild confusion confronts them, Roberts having tried unsuccessfully to borrow evening clothes that fitted him. Amy Campbell, however, says that no one will know that Agnes put the suit away, but Willis Campbell is less reassuring.

> Campbell: "Oh, indeed! *Won't* they? When Baker and Merrick meet at the club, and exchange notes about Agnes locking up Roberts' clothes. . . ."
> Mrs. Roberts, with horror: "Edward! you didn't send that word to them!"
> Roberts: "Why—why—I'm afraid we did, something like it, my dear. We had to explain our request, somehow."
> Mr. Roberts, relaxing into a chair: "Then I simply never can hold up my head again."
> (She lets it fall in typical despair.)

This was indeed an age when saying and doing the *correct* thing were of paramount importance and Howells represents to perfection this particular phase of the life around him. A breach of etiquette was a much worse misdemeanor than it is today—or at least it was looked upon as being much more serious. There was also an air of reserve and formality that, to a certain extent, has broken down. No matter how excited the ladies may be in Howells' plays, especially in *The Mouse Trap*, they never for a moment lose their sense of propriety. If they did, much of the real humor would be gone from the plays, while certainly much of the charm would be missing. The characters are all perfectly secure in their station of life and one always has the feeling that Howells would not have them otherwise. But he does enjoy poking fun at the superficial qualities of convention that are always prevalent in any age, and shows that unless you adopt them you might as well sign your own death certificate. Happily, Howells does this from a purely humorous, not a satiric viewpoint, which is one of many qualities that contribute to the success of these plays.

Howells' influence was most important upon later writers, for he set the example of presenting everyday people in everyday life, while the social ease with which his characters conduct themselves set a standard.   Both in his novels and in his plays he proved definitively that what is going on immediately around us is interesting, and both dramatists and novelists studied his works for their honest portrayals of real people, for their revelation of natural action, and for their unstudied ease in dialogue.   Under no circumstances will the characters in his plays infringe upon the standards which order their lives but at the same time there is, of course, no conscious effort on their part to avoid doing so— their standards are a part of them.   Very rightly did Clyde Fitch, upon whom Howells had an important influence, call this "The Howells Age."

During this period Brander Matthews, who collaborated with Bronson Howard in writing *Peter Stuyvesant,* wrote two comedies; *This Picture and That* and *The Decision of the Court.*   Of no great importance, they are entertaining and possess a certain amount of charm.   The first deals with a widow who is devoted to the memory of her dead husband, whom she thought the model of perfection, until she is informed of his unfaithfulness to her. When she finds this out she accepts the hand of the man who is in love with her.   The plot, trifling as it is, is cleverly worked out, and the widow's attempts to conceal her interest in her suitor are deftly drawn touches.   *The Decision of the Court,* which reveals the love of two people for each other, although they have never agreed upon anything, is a very clever play.   They are awaiting the divorce decree and when it comes decide to remarry and go away together.   However, this is a play which we shall discuss later.

Our Best Society, adapted in 1875 by Irving Browne from George W. Curtis' *Potiphar Papers,* is a play which strongly resembles *Self, Wheat and Chaff,* and the plays of the earlier period.   It is a caricature, the people in it types, while the main object is satire.   Reverend Cream Cheese—the name of one of the characters—is sufficient to indicate what we may expect from the play.

Edgar Fawcett's *Buntling Ball* (1884), is described as a "Graeco-American Play.   Being a Poetical Satire on New York Society."   It may be a poetical satire but it is certainly a curiosity, which is at once evident from the dramatis personae, which includes a Chorus of Knickerbocker Young Men, Maneuvering Mammas, Social Strugglers, Belles, Wallflowers, Gossips, Anglomaniacs, Gluttons, and a character with the alliterative name of Florimel Filagree! For its sheer strangeness alone the play is mentioned, otherwise it may be consigned to oblivion.

There is probably no period in the history of American manners in which social life was surrounded with the same glittering aura as it was during the Gilded Age. Mrs. Astor reigned supreme with a queenly dignity unmatched by any of her rivals. In fact, those who made the greatest efforts to rival her were generally outside of the charmed circle of the "four hundred" and felt that they must make a spectacular display in order to win recognition. Not until the Vanderbilts finally gave so elaborate a ball that no one could resist going did Mrs. Astor finally call upon them and leave her card. Up until that time she had steadfastly refused to notice them. This marked the beginning of the end for the reign of Mrs. Astor. After that she had to acknowledge that she had rivals who could and did attract the circle over which she had presided for so long a time. Huge fortunes were spent on balls more elaborate than any that have ever been held since. At first these functions seemed little better than bad investments for those who were giving them but gradually they were responsible for the breaking up of what was one of the most exclusive social groups in America. Everyone turned out for them and New York could no longer boast of a "four hundred."

C. THE ESTABLISHMENT OF SOCIAL COMEDY— CLYDE FITCH

So far, with a few exceptions, notably Tyler's *Contrast,* some of Howard's plays, the adaptations of Daly and the one act plays of Howells, what passed for the comedy of manners in America was largely social satire. But finally, after what seems to have been a long preparation for him, Clyde Fitch definitely established social comedy in America. With his advent, realism in action, detail and dialogue came into their own. The very human and natural qualities that we find in his plays seem to have burst upon the public, for unhappily very few of Howells' one act plays were produced professionally. In general, with a few exceptions, the characters in the plays which came before Fitch's time *represented* certain kinds of people; they were not the people themselves, but in the dramas of Fitch the characters are real human beings. For instance, a social climber does not merely represent the class to which she belongs, she lives as an individual before us and it is as an individual that we are interested in her. Fitch's objective was not satire but it was to present us with honest pictures of life. Gifted with an almost uncanny sense of what was good theatre, he wrote his plays primarily for the stage, and not with the idea that they were to be handed down as great literature. But while the dramatic effect came first, one cannot say that Fitch's plays are not good literature. He was too careful a craftsman to be slipshod in his composition, and he knew that a careless usage of expression would ruin a play. Consequently, his plays were, except in a few instances, successful. The natural tone and easy flow of the dialogue and the swift repartee frequently bordering upon brilliance, assure his dramatic work an unquestioned place in American literature.

The period during which Fitch wrote his plays is one of the most interesting in the history of American manners. The rush of newcomers to New York had broken down what had once seemed invincible barriers. The old New York social order composed of a few powerful families around whom clustered a less influential—though not less self-esteemed group—had at last proved vulnerable to the vast horde of new rich people who invaded the stronghold. These old families in many instances could no longer afford to ignore this new class, satisfying as it would have been. They needed money to maintain their mode of living, and while they never accepted these people in their hearts, ostensibly they seemed to have done so. Consequently, the period from 1890-1910 was one which witnessed a strange assemblage of persons at social functions; functions which, not so very much earlier, would have been extremely exclusive. Those days were over when New Yorkers occasionally permitted themselves to smile at their own rigid customs; when because they turned their backs upon something distasteful to them, that something ceased to exist. No longer did everyone know everyone else. New York had become cosmopolitan in its social life as well as in its business life. Consequently, Fitch lived in what might be called a kaleidoscopic period, and one which was intensely alive. This was exactly what he liked. One has only to read his letters to see how keenly interested he was in every phase of life around him. His energy was apparently unbounded; his capacity for work remarkable. The frequency with which he crossed the Atlantic ocean amounted almost to commuting.

His familiarity with the Continent, and his ability to interpret Continental social customs are evident in his work. The fact that he never stood in awe of anyone or anything gives to his plays an ease that definitely contributes to their success. They reflect the quality of perfect social assurance. His good humored satire springs from his sharp observation and understanding of the life and people around him.

We have only to consider the range of Fitch's plays to appreciate his familiarity with his subjects. His own account of his method in writing an historical play is revealing to anyone who may wonder at his accuracy in grasping the atmosphere of another day and age. He read and digested every possible account of the period in which he proposed to set his play, and then with the aid of his lively imagination he was able to interpret a very real and convincing atmosphere.

His plays fit into most of the phases of American social comedy which we shall later discuss. *Beau Brummell* (1890), *His Grace de Grammont* (1894), and *Barbara Frietchie* (1899), reflect the social scene of the past. *The Stubbornness of Geraldine* (1902), and *Her Great Match* (1905), are examples of the international contrast. *The Girl with the Green Eyes* (1902), and *The Truth* (1906), display the conflict between society and the individual. *A Modern Match* (1892), and *The Climbers* (1901) reflect both the relations that exist between society and the institutions of marriage and divorce, and the interrelations between society and business. *The Stubbornness of Geraldine* and *Her Own Way* (1903) are sympathetic and understanding studies of the conflict between society and love.

Because Clyde Fitch loved life and was interested in everything around him his plays reflect almost exactly his own times. They are, in regard to this particular matter, contemporaneous, and so are of keen interest to the social historian. In so far as plot and motive are concerned they are universal. Although fundamentally not satiric, they contain biting irony when Fitch is exposing certain types of individuals or is ridiculing some foolish notion that happened to have caught the public eye. Were we to study each of his plays in turn we should gain a very good idea of what it was fashionable to say during this or that season, of what songs were the most popular, of the topics most discussed, of the changes in interior decoration, and along with these superficial aspects of life we have the more fundamental interests and laws of society as well. Whatever Fitch saw or heard was for him dramatic material.

Most important of all is the complete understanding of social values that Fitch displays. Never is there any uncertainty in his social comedies of the essential laws upon which society is based. The actions of his characters are governed by the creeds which order their lives. Always we are aware of the social scene which forms the background of the plot. In *The Climbers* New York society is actually the moving force which causes the characters to behave as they do. We see the struggle on the part of several individuals to try to break through the social barrier. Another tries to be a financial king. In contrast to these people are those who need make no effort. The cold contempt in which society holds a climber is skillfully portrayed. The very compactness of New York society looms up like a massive granite wall behind the action of the play. If anyone can scale the wall by virtue of wealth or wit, or both, it is greatly to his or her credit, but the spectacle of the struggle, whether success or failure results, is generally amusing. The varied assortment of characters moving side by side throughout *The Climbers* offers an excellent contrast. Fitch shows great subtlety here, the distinction between these people being unusually fine. We see how, through an unfortunate marriage on someone's part, society had to swallow a bitter pill. That the pill was *very* bitter is plainly seen in a conversation between Ruth Hunter and her sister-in-law, Blanche. After the funeral of Blanche's husband the will is read and there is no money. Blanche then shows herself in her true colors and Ruth can at last tell her exactly what she and her friends have always thought of her. Had it not been for her brother's sake, Ruth would have made no attempt to do anything for his wife. In fact, she would never have met her, if her brother had not brought her into the family. The situation is a very common one, but Fitch deals with it in an unusually effective and realistic manner. It is just such natural events which occur during the course of life that he knew so well how to present.

The remarkable settings for *The Climbers*—perfect in every detail—won wide admiration for the author who attended to this phase of production with infinite care. His eye for artistic detail was exceptionally acute—detail both in dress and in stage setting. There were never any glaring incongruities in his setting which have so often marred an otherwise admirable production.

His tastes, inherited and acquired, were well established, so that it is not surprising that he dealt largely with social comedy. Besides, the superficial fancies which swept society then as now delighted him and appealed to his sense of humor. One cannot imagine him wandering the back streets to glean material for a play, although had he decided to do so the result would very likely have been successful. What he liked, however, as we can see from his letters, was the more agreeable side of life. It appealed to his aesthetic sense and suited his personality. Furthermore, he had grown up in an atmosphere of refinement. His mother loved social life with all of its fuss and show, and Fitch, being very much under her surveillance as a boy, naturally found himself a part of it. When he finally left home and struck out for himself, what he had heard and observed for many years formed a vast store of knowledge upon which he could draw. He had only to tap his own memory for a real and true portrayal of a character. Judging from the many humorous and ironic comments which he makes upon contemporary society, one suspects that these observations had been bottled up for a long time and were waiting for an outlet. They did not fall upon barren soil, certainly, as we can readily see from his plays. It is said that Fitch thoroughly enjoyed making a remark to set the ball rolling in a conversation with his friends and then to sit back to both watch and listen to the results of what he had begun. Here again is evidence of his dramatic sense and his grasp of situation. It was situation more than anything else which always made an instantaneous impression upon him—particularly a comic one. Professedly, Fitch preferred only a few close friends, but he had an extraordinarily wide circle of acquaintances and was an excellent judge of human character. As a whole he judges his audiences equally well which may be another reason for his success in the field of social comedy. To go to the theatre in his day was regarded more strictly as a social event than it is today. Consequently, social comedy appealed to a larger element in the audience.

Clyde Fitch's influence upon the playwrights who succeeded him and upon the American theatre is hard to calculate. First of all, it is because of his accurate presentation of life that the drama today is more truthful and closer to fact than it was before he began to write. The relation between society and individual human beings became of foremost interest to many dramatists, who studied Fitch's methods in his two finest plays, *The Girl with the Green Eyes* and *The Truth*. The inherent weaknesses of the two central characters, namely, jealousy and inability to tell the truth, are stimulated constantly by social custom. This is particularly evident in *The Truth* where the so-called "white lies" which are a part of daily life, contribute to Becky Warder's inherited tendency toward deception. It is this revelation of human behavior controlled by outside forces which makes Fitch so important.

Because he did succeed so well in this particular field the public began to demand better plays on the part of American dramatists, a demand that they could not afford to ignore. Consequently, the whole level of our native drama became higher and, added to this, accuracy and good taste in stage settings became prime essentials. Moreover, Fitch was an important influence in arousing the interest of American playwrights in native material.

D. THE NEW CENTURY

Although the work of Clyde Fitch covers approximately the years from 1890 to 1910 we have placed his name under The Establishment of Social Comedy, and shall call the period following him The New Century which includes the work of Augustus Thomas, Langdon Mitchell, Jesse Lynch Williams, A. E. Thomas, Anne Crawford Flexner, Louis K. Anspacher, Thompson Buchanan and Clare Kummer. Of these dramatists Mitchell, Williams and A. E. Thomas have made the most important contributions to American social comedy.

With *The New York Idea* of Mitchell, the comedy of manners in America reached a zenith, for this play is still regarded by many critics as the most brilliant of our comedies, and when we read the play the almost incomparable swiftness of the dialogue makes us care very little about the plot which is conventional and of no great importance. In fact, the play depends largely upon the dialogue which might almost be said to hold it together. The problem around which Mitchell weaves his play is one that belongs to a phase of social comedy and, in so far as this particular matter is concerned, he has done a thorough job. Satire and irony abound throughout, but the play remains purely a comedy of manners of the very highest order. It was for its time startlingly modern, and like the plays of Williams, far in advance of its day. The lightness with which divorce is regarded, in fact the extreme lightness with which the characters regard life as a whole is the theme of the play.

If *The New York Idea* was advanced in thought for its day, *Why Marry?* and *Why Not?* by Jesse Lynch Williams created a furor. The former, produced in New York in 1917, at first shocked audiences into a state of silent and severe disapproval until they suddenly saw the humor which lies behind the plot. From what were bold discussions of divorce presented by earlier dramatists, Williams proceeds to entertain the idea of companionate marriage. This play astonished an unsuspecting public, for while the subject of trial marriage was not new, it had certainly not been handled by a playwright in so frank and startling a manner. However, the brilliant dialogue and unfailing humor combined with the fact that the characters are people with a sense of fitness, won over the public after the first jolt had worn away. The play is an outstanding example of the use of social comedy as a means to rid society of a destructive force.

When *Why Not?* was produced in 1922, the public was more hardened to new ideas, and the very modern theme did not produce so startling an effect. However, the play is again an example of advanced thinking on the part of a playwright, and it provides a remedy for a situation which is very common but which generally brings disaster to the people involved. It is a pity that we do not have a number of prominent dramatists who could present before their audiences in Williams' fashion the logical solution to problems which keep society in a constant state of unrest.

Many of the leading dramatists of this period deal with the ever increasing difficulties which tend to destroy modern marriage. A. E. Thomas' *Her Husband's Wife,* and *The Rainbow* are both concerned with marriage. While the former seems very light and at first glance may not appear to have any serious thought behind it, it actually attacks a very real and important phase of life—the tendency toward hypochondria which fascinates so many people. Numberless are the homes which are habitually wrapped in a mantle of gloom because the mistress of the household is too delicate to see anyone, or to glance at the other sex, because her lord and master cannot stand any excitement or gaiety. *Her Husband's Wife* is a bright and lively, but none the less effective, treatment of a very definite social evil. Its almost farcical mood is in strong contrast to the serious study of marriage and divorce which we find in Thomas' *The Rainbow.*

The Better Understanding, which Thomas wrote in collaboration with Clayton Hamilton is again a serious problem play and one which falls into the category of comedy only because of the technical definition of comedy. In this play as well as in the ones just mentioned, and in such works as *A Woman's Way* by Thompson Buchanan and *The Marriage Game* of Anne Crawford Flexner we are aware of the ever increasing complexity of contemporary life. Louis K. Anspacher goes a step further when he introduces the laboring class into his play, *The Unchastened Woman*. In this particular instance we depart from the field of social comedy to a certain extent, for there are two totally different themes presented.

Despite the fact that Clyde Fitch is regarded as having established American social comedy, there is a great advance in this field when we consider the plays just mentioned. There is in the plays of Fitch what is now looked upon as "old-fashioned" sentiment, and one must admit that this becomes rather thick at times, but in the plays of the authors who come during the next period there is very little sentimentality, or perhaps it is better to say that sentimentality is concealed under a more worldly conduct. The social comedies of Augustus Thomas do not usually deal with any particular problem in society but are charming comedies whose main interest is a good story. And this is true of the comedies of Clare Kummer. They are charming because of their gay and carefree atmosphere. What sets Mrs. Kummer's plays apart, however, is the breezy attitude of so many of her characters. They never seem concerned with life in the same serious way that other people are. They plunge wholeheartedly into the wildest of schemes and as a rule come out with only a surface scratch or two. This does not say that they are not aware of their responsibilities to society—they are simply so completely assured that they never have to think at all. Very few playwrights have succeeded in imparting so wholly a delightful atmosphere in their plays as has Clare Kummer.

The new century, when one stops for a moment to view it, has two definite aspects in the field of social comedy. On the one hand we have the purely entertaining plays of Augustus Thomas and Clare Kummer, while on the other are the social comedies with a definitely serious theme. In the majority of cases the playwrights were reflecting the steadily growing responsibilities that have come with each period in American life. Already, as we have seen, what is termed the "old order" in American social life had broken down in many instances. What is called "Society" had expanded far beyond the proportions with which the past century was familiar. By this time, many of the difficulties of entering into circles which were once impregnable had been swept away. This was owing largely to the tremendous expansion of business which brought great wealth to many people who previously were unknown. Now they could live in the same manner as those whom they had envied, and in many instances they far outshone them. Their money was useful and they became a part of the social life to which they had always aspired.

During this period of social readjustment women came to the fore and assumed a position that they had never occupied before. They handled many matters, both domestic and in the field of business, that formerly only a man was supposed to consider. It is because of this revolution in society that we find so many of the important social comedies dealing with the relations between society and the institutions of marriage and divorce.

E. POST-WAR COMEDY

When America entered the World War woman could perform so many active services that her place became assured alongside of men. After the war one could hardly imagine the women who had taken a prominent part in its activities both here and abroad, settling back into a secondary place. They had proved themselves efficient in every conceivable capacity and were now perfectly free to enter into public life with no stigma whatever attached to them. This, of course, added new problems to the already bewildering turmoil that resulted from the world wide conflict. Thus we find the playwrights of the post war period of comedy dealing with the question of careers for women, and what happens to their husbands and children when they are left to their own devices. Out of this grew logically enough the amazing freedom with which the younger generation decided its own course of life. This reached the proportions of an upheaval, and so swiftly did it come that parents were left gasping. Appalled and horrified, they strove in vain to re-establish their traditional jurisdiction over the actions of their children.

Practically all of the dramatists who come under consideration during this period have a serious outlook upon life, and while

39

their comedies are in many instances bubbling over with a rich humor and contain characters who afford plenty of comic relief, their purpose is nearly always serious. This is undoubtedly because of the increasing complexity of modern life which we have already noted. The new problems which confront us must be met and overcome, or at least understood. Rachel Crothers, Philip Barry, James Forbes, Gilbert Emery and S. N. Behrman all have something very definite to say. They are not writing for the sheer sake of amusement. Among the topics which these playwrights discuss are the revolt of the younger generation, the difficulty of readjustment after the war for those who had been over seas, the increasing strain that modern life has imposed upon marriage, and finally the introduction of radical ideas, or at least a discussion of them which we find in the social comedies of S. N. Behrman. With this particular playwright we seem to have the greatest departure of all from what has generally held the center of attraction in comedies of this type.

Whether one is reluctant to accept the raising of these questions in social comedy is no longer a matter for dispute. The fact that they are today widely discussed in every path of life is evident. Behrman's plays simply reflect new problems which confront society. It is hard to correlate social comedy with discussions of socialism and communism, but since matters of this kind *are* being talked about by people who at one time never gave them a thought, it is only natural to find them in our contemporary plays. It is another example of the interrelation between the drama and society. The question as to whether a playwright anticipates public thought or reflects it, has never been settled and probably never can be. This is because the theatre and contemporary life are so closely allied. An outstanding dramatist frequently does contribute new ideas, while another will gather together his material from his observations and present it as logically and clearly as possible. Both are contributing to the enlightenment of the public. The theatre and life go hand in hand which makes it impossible to say definitely that the drama either reflects or leads public thought. Each derives something from the other.

More and more has American social comedy tended to depart from what may be called pure comedy of manners, for an audience today seems to prefer some particular problem to be discussed rather than to spend the evening witnessing a play based upon a solely artificial convention. There have been very few comedies of this latter type in America, William Dean Howells' *Unexpected Guests* being the most perfect example of this genre. Here, as we have seen, the action depends entirely upon the resourcefulness of the hostess as to whether or not she can live up to the superficial demands made by polite society. Entertaining and brilliant as the play is, no serious motive lies behind it. This same trend away from pure comedy of manners has taken place in other countries. In France and England especially there was more light, conventional comedy than there ever was in this country, largely because Americans have always seemed to have a preference for drama that contained a theme reflecting some contemporary question that is of general interest. Consequently, the majority of our comedies have been interspersed with political, business, and domestic matters, and yet we may certainly say that in the plays which have made their mark in the history of American social comedy there are comparatively few which are so contemporaneous in tone that they have become outmoded or unintelligible. This is partly because the dramatists have been wise enough to use a universal theme for the basis of the plot, and partly because, as we have already indicated, social laws and values do not change so radically as economic or political conditions.

That society in the narrow sense of the word, has broken down to a certain extent we have pointed out. The plays of Miss Crothers like *Nice People* (1920), *Expressing Willie* (1924), and *Let Us Be Gay* (1929), reveal what is now termed "café society." This particular element is noted for its restless search for pleasure and for its conspicuous place in the public eye. At first it was composed largely of young people but today it is obvious that anyone who has the necessary physical endurance, and who can provide "originality" is a welcome member. The "café set" is very elastic indeed, but quite as proud of its superficial achievements as the more conservative element composed largely of Junior

League members. These two factions are waging a battle for social supremacy, for not since the days of Mrs. Astor has there been a well organized social group which could claim undisputed leadership. The Junior League emphasizes a worthwhile purpose, and the question of family background is of great importance. A member must devote a certain amount of her time to some worthy cause. Her association with the League does not depend upon how much money she has, nor upon the number of times her picture appears in the papers. To refer again to Miss Crothers' work, one might say that Teddy in *Nice People* shifts from the careless attitude of "café society" to the more serious outlook of the Junior League. The Seton family in Philip Barry's *Holiday* belong most definitely to the more reserved group whose daughters become League members, for here it is quite strictly a question of family. Notoriety which arises from unconventional escapades is frowned upon and generally avoided. On the other hand, a few of the strict barriers have collapsed for today a girl may go on the stage and still keep her name in the social register. She may go into business and yet retain her social position. Her freedom in these matters has caused many new problems which our present day playwrights are constantly bringing before us.

James Forbes's *The Famous Mrs. Fair* (1920), and Gilbert Emery's *Episode* (1925), both disclose the disastrous effect that complete absorption in a career may have upon marriage. It is interesting to consider these two plays together for *The Famous Mrs. Fair* deals with a woman who takes her family for granted, and *Episode* draws the picture of a man who has taken his wife for granted. In each case the awakening comes as a terrible shock, and only after irreparable damage has been done. Both of these plays are fine illustrations of the serious vein that runs through American social comedy. *Episode* is hardly comedy at all from one viewpoint for technically the ending is not what might be termed a happy one. *The Famous Mrs. Fair* ends satisfactorily for everyone, including the audience, but it closes on a serious note. This, however, is one of the salient characteristics in the field of American social comedy. It is bound up with the fundamental questions of life and is seldom concerned with sheer amusement.

One of the most notable differences in the post war comedy from that of earlier times is the lessening of contrasts between the characters. This has arisen from the breaking down of standards which began noticeably around the turn of the century, and which was greatly accelerated by the World War. Characters who formerly exemplified types of people not acceptable now mingle freely with those who are representative of established society. For instance, Kitty Brown, a leading character in Rachel Crothers' *Let Us Be Gay,* is not only a divorcée but she has taken up a business career, either of which would have constituted a social stigma at an earlier period while the combination would have spelled complete disaster. Today, very little thought is given to either of these matters by society as a whole. Miss Crothers presents a varied group of persons in *Let Us Be Gay,* all of whom accept each other with absolute nonchalance. What each was or is makes practically no difference to the others because all of them are guests of the dowager, Mrs. Boucicault.

Another outgrowth of the breakdown in standards is the freedom in present day use of words compared with the comparatively limited vocabulary employed before the end of the nineteenth century. Slang, within limits, is no longer regarded as vulgar or common but as rather attractive. Frequently, it gives the dialogue of a play a certain intimacy not found in the earlier plays. No better examples of "nice" slang exist than those in Philip Barry's plays. They abound in dialogue full of really delightful and refreshing bits of slang which add to rather than detract from their charm. This freedom in speech has widened in a certain manner the scope for a writer of social comedy. Before its advent the writer of social comedy was far more limited in his choice of language. Some of today's expressions would undoubtedly have shocked audiences of an earlier period while certainly they would have been considered totally inappropriate for social comedy. Now, however, an audience would indulge in a tolerant, if not superior, smile at the very proper phraseology of "olden times." This expansion in vocabulary naturally accompanies the greater freedom in action that exists today. The two are inseparable.

Until the plays of the dramatists who belong to this post war period of social comedy, the *New York Idea* of Langdon Mitchell, and *Why Marry?* and *Why Not?* of Jesse Lynch Williams were probably the three most outspoken social comedies to deal with the questions of marriage and divorce. Williams's *Why Marry?* as we have already seen, startled audiences at first. These three plays, at least, broke away from the strictly conventional dialogue and action that had prevailed. Consequently, the marital tangles with which Miss Crothers, Gilbert Emery, James Forbes and Philip Barry deal, do not startle us although Mr. Emery in a letter to the author of this thesis, states that audiences were evidently not prepared to accept the frank handling of the situation presented in *Episode*. This is a great pity and is certainly a reflection upon any audience which might pride itself upon being either intelligent or sophisticated or both. It is seldom that so fine a play comes before us.

The post war social comedies in America delve more deeply into the underlying motives that disrupt social life. Playwrights are no longer satisfied to show only the results of some disturbing factor, but they now pry far below the surface. Consequently, their work has become more vital, and in many instances is of invaluable assistance in helping people to understand difficult problems. The plays in the particular field in which we are interested are generally more thought-provoking than they formerly were. Full of sprightly wit and lively humor as they are, nevertheless there are very few that are written without serious intent. It is generally to farce that we must turn today if we seek only light amusement. American society is too closely linked with business and money making to be shown as remaining aloof from these matters. Naturally, it is these matters which cause our innumerable problems and which ultimately establish our standards.

The fact that women with unquestionable social position may prefer a public career rather than a comparatively idle existence, goes back to the industrial revolution. Their new activities have added to the unsettling influences upon the social life in this country. For even though a woman may not choose some outside activity, the very fact that she is free to do so, gives her a feeling of independence which was once unknown. It is hardly possible to find one play among the outstanding comedies of contemporary playwrights that does not portray its feminine characters on an equal footing with the male ones.

In the wake of this change in society has come one of equal importance. The young people of today are far more enlightened as to their elders' doings than they ever were before. For instance, a daughter no longer has in her mother the example she once had. Her mother comes and goes as she pleases; she has any number of interests which have nothing to do with her home. Consequently, the girl feels free to do as she pleases and, for a short period of time after the war, she surpassed herself. However, since that particular era has passed by, a more intelligent outlook prevails.

CHAPTER II

The Phases of American Social Comedy

A. THE INTERNATIONAL CONTRAST

One of the most interesting phases in American social life is the international contrast which begins with the first native comedy to be produced professionally, *The Contrast* (1787), and runs through each period to the present day. The difference in the treatment employed by the playwrights during each of the periods of comedy is indicative of the changes that have taken place in social life itself. The international contrast began with the caricature of the Anglomaniac in Tyler's *Contrast* and emerges with the perfectly natural representation of a foreign character. Of course, this phase of American social comedy is not confined to the contrasting of individuals, but it also contrasts the conflicting fundamental ideas of two nations which Bronson Howard presented very well in *One of Our Girls* and *Kate;* Clyde Fitch in *Her Great Match* and S. N. Behrman in *Rain from Heaven.* This aspect of the international contrast is the more important one because it reveals the basic differences that distinguish one nation from another. It shows the conflicting viewpoints of society, the difference in the moral standards, the clash of temperaments.

The Contrast, produced April 16th, 1787, at the John Street Theatre, New York, showed plainly what was the attitude of America toward England at that period. Not only does the caricature of an American whose god is Lord Chesterfield reveal the general antipathy felt, but the constant emphasis upon solid, native worth and common sense shows that Tyler was advising Americans to turn their backs upon England and to rely upon themselves. The two characters who illustrate these decidedly different sides of life are Colonel Manly and Dimple. To heighten this contrast Tyler presents us with their respective servants, Jonathan and Jessamy. As the New England Yankee, ignorant but shrewd,

45

Jonathan became the prototype for one of the favorite American stage characters whose popularity lasted far into the nineteenth century. Of course, Jonathan has no manners or polish, but he is sensible and upright. Jessamy, Dimple's servant, is, on the contrary, imbued with all the mannerisms of the elegant gentleman and reads portions of Lord Chesterfield's letters to his master whenever the latter feels the need of a bit of coaching. The meeting between the two servants at once shows the fundamental contrast upon which the play is based. Jonathan refuses to be called a servant by Jessamy, whom he mistakes for a gentleman. When he tells Jessamy this, the latter replies:

> —"Give me leave to say, I wonder then at your familiarity."
>
> Jonathan: "Why, as to the matter of that, Mr.—pray, what's your name?"
>
> Jessamy: "Jessamy, at your service."
>
> Jonathan: "Why, I swear we don't make any great matter of distinction in our state, between quality and other folks."
>
> Jessamy: "This is, indeed, a levelling principle. I hope, Mr. Jonathan, you have not taken part with the insurgents."

The contrast between Colonel Manly and Dimple is evident when the two men are conversing in the apartment of Charlotte Manly, the colonel's sister.

> Dimple: —"Colonel, I presume you have been in Europe?"
>
> Manly: "Indeed, Sir, I was never ten leagues from the continent."
>
> Dimple: "Believe me, Colonel, you have an immense pleasure to come; and when you have seen the brilliant exhibitions of Europe, you will learn to despise the amusements of this country as much as I do."
>
> Manly: "Therefore I do not wish to see them; for I can never esteem that knowledge valuable, which tends to give me a distaste for my native country."

Herein lies the raison d'etre of the play. The ridiculous affectation of Dimple and the frank honesty of Manly come before us constantly. Of course, Dimple turns out to be a philanderer of the worst type but not until Charlotte Manly and Letitia, ward of Charlotte's uncle, have made fools of themselves over him. The conversations between Charlotte and Letitia are filled with references to the fashionable customs and amusements of the day. Strolling in the Mall, or along the Battery, paying morning visits (mainly to glean as much gossip as possible), attending the theatre where between acts one eats oranges and nuts, the formal politeness (which Charlotte ridicules), the evening entertainments at private homes, are all mentioned casually. These two girls, especially Charlotte, are excellent portrayals of the coquette of that period, and when they discuss the methods to ensnare the unsuspecting male, it is obvious that no new tricks have been discovered.

What is of especial interest in the field of social comedy is that Charlotte, Letitia, Maria, their friend, and Colonel Manly are characters whose social position is so completely assured that no question of doubt can possibly arise, but with a few rare exceptions the characters we meet in subsequent plays until about 1860 are of the parvenu type. Royall Tyler was unquestionably a man of culture so that when he wrote *The Contrast* it was natural for him to present a picture of the people he knew best. Because he is so perfectly sure of himself, he makes no effort whatever to establish the social atmosphere in which his characters move but strikes at once the note of high comedy. As already pointed out, the fact that Tyler makes Manly an *officer* prevents any question of that character's standing, for it was the only profession in America at that time which implied social security. The clerical profession had begun to lose its social preeminence, and the physician and the lawyer had not yet established their social standing as professional men.

The next play in which we find an international contrast of note is *Fashion,* by Mrs. Mowatt, produced in 1845, although James Nelson Barker in *Tears and Smiles* (1807), had poked fun at the French vogue in America when he created a character, Fluttermore, who returns from Europe literally encrusted in an artificial polish. Without this Continental glitter, Fluttermore considers a person hopeless, while he despises both Americans and America.

In Mrs. Mowatt's *Fashion,* however, we have depicted a perfect rage for the French way of doing a thing, not on the part of socially established families but on the part of the parvenu like Mrs. Tiffany.   Count Jolimaître is visiting America and Mrs. Tiffany has snatched him up as the prospective husband for her daughter, Seraphina.   Unfortunately, the "Count" turns out to be a crook well known to the police in both France and England and his station in life has never been above that of a valet.   Before all this comes to light, however, Mrs. Tiffany hangs upon his every word, stands in awe of him and fairly grovels in his presence. Millinette, a French maid in her employ, knows the "Count" for what he really is, but does not betray him.   It is to Millinette that Mrs. Tiffany turns for knowledge of both the French language and French customs.   Her butchering of the French language sends the maid into fits of laughter but she flatters her mistress upon her ability.   Millinette, however, remains free from caricature unless one considers the extremely broken English which Mrs. Mowatt makes her speak.   The role of a French mother which Mrs. Tiffany assumes is one of the most amusing touches in the play.   However, what Mrs. Mowatt was stressing was the desire on the part of people who wished to become social leaders, to be *fashionable,* to take up whatever happened to be the vogue, regardless of what it was, and the international contrast here simply arises because at that particular time French customs were the desired objective.

The influence of *Fashion* lasted for several generations.   There was during this period a great deal of friction between *native* playwrights and the dramatic critics but Mrs. Mowatt seems to have conquered the latter, for the critic of "Albion," a leading journal, called *Fashion* the best American comedy in existence, while the "Herald" remarked upon its enthusiastic reception by an audience which contained all the "literati" of the city and many of the "élite."[1]   Mr. Hutton suggests that an interesting play might have arisen out of the Herald's distinction between the "literati" and the "élite," and when one considers this possibility, it *does* seem

---

[1] Hutton, *Curiosities of the American Stage,* p. 59.

a shame that some playwright did not grasp at the idea.   The fact that Mrs. Mowatt's play presented a picture of American home life and won favor from the critics is notable, for there was a strong prejudice against native scenes.   In 1857 Mrs. Sidney Bateman's play *The Golden Calf; or Marriage à la Mode* laid its scenes in London and Paris, while William Henry Hurlburt's play *Americans in Paris* hardly needs to have the geographical position pointed out.

Mrs. Bateman's *The Golden Calf; or Marriage à la Mode* begins with its scene laid in London where we meet Edward L'Estrange, who is in love with Alethea Arkwright but because he is poor feels that he cannot ask her hand in marriage.   He plans to elope with Lady Hebe Haugh, estranged wife of Sir Stephen Haugh, because she has turned to him and has aroused his sympathy.   These four people, Edward and Alethea, who are American, and Lord and Lady Haugh, English subjects, are socially assured but into their group comes Crassus Stearine, Esquire, with his daughter, Pollie Ann Maria Stearine, whom he hopes will be able to acquire a title by reason of the Stearine money.   These two characters are so hopelessly crude and newly rich that one cannot call their presence in the play an international contrast because the contrast is not between people socially of the same class.   What is of particular interest about the play is the fact that it may be the first time that a realistic play of American life had a foreign setting.   Perhaps Mrs. Bateman's father, Joseph Cowell, suggested the setting for he was an Englishman by birth, and had been a low comedian on the English stage.   An amusing character is Colonel Philanto Parasite, who trails after Miss Rosalie Ricketts, aunt of Edward L'Estrange, hoping that he may eventually marry her for her money.   This he finally does but as the plot turns out, she is divested of her money which falls into Edward's possession.

William Henry Hurlburt's *Americans in Paris* (1858) is a much better play which preserves the tone of the comedy of manners throughout.   In a very gay and sparkling play we are introduced to two American couples, Arthur and Amelia Morris and Doctor and Annie Botherer.   A masqued ball is the high spot of the comedy when Arthur, who is carrying on an affair behind his wife's back, says to her, thinking she is someone else, that since his wife is not French she doesn't believe that all men are deceivers by nature. This, of course, draws a contrast between the French and American viewpoint of a married man's behavior. A fifth character is M. Lamouret, a philandering Frenchman, with practically no moral scruples at all who is the source of much amusement, because of the jealousy he arouses. Dr. Botherer's solicitous attitude toward his wife is a guise for keeping her under his eye, but she manages to enjoy the masqued ball and at the same time to save the situation for Amelia and Arthur. The fundamental contrast lies in the different way in which Americans and the French regard marriage and all that it implies, and Hurlburt brings out this point with skill and understanding.

Augustin Daly's *Our English Friend,* adapted in 1882 from *Reif von Reiflingen* by Gustav von Moser, was one of the first plays in which a dramatist does not caricature an Englishman. The scene of the play is a hunting lodge at Cutty Corners in Northern New York where a young married couple is giving a week-end house party. The wives, feeling neglected, and being certain that their husbands are flirting, decide to test the depth of the male affection by asking them not to go hunting. Of course, the men go and the wives are wretched but retaliate by arousing their jealousy over the Englishman, Digby de Rigby. The latter's confusion over the strange behavior going on around him forms one of the main sources for amusement in the play, but the importance of this character lies in the fact that Daly created a character from another country without affectation and one with a high sense of honor—in other words—a gentleman.

One of the most humorous angles in the play lies in the contrast between the urban week-end guests and the village folk of Cutty Corners. The very prim ways of the latter make an amusing distinction between them and the more cosmopolitan persons. All of the characters are well drawn, from Mrs. Cornelia Partradge, symbol of the passing Victorian Age, to her niece, Barbie Vaughn, who heralds the modern young woman.

An interesting play in which the scene is laid in France is Bronson Howard's *One of Our Girls* (1885), in which Kate Shipley, an American girl, goes to visit her French cousins, the Fonblanques. Their amazement over her travelling unchaperoned is in violent contrast to their plans for marrying their own daughter to a notorious roué. Always sheltered during her maidenhood, Julie Fonblanque feels that after marriage she will be free and this again shows the difference between the French and American conception of marriage. Kate Shipley's frankness and her ability to manage her own love affair shock Madame Fonblanque to the core. In fact, everyone she meets, except Captain Gregory, the Englishman whom she eventually marries, looks upon her as barbaric. There is in this play a complete lack of understanding on the part of the French people, that because of an essential decency in Americans they can carry on a courtship before marriage without the necessity of a chaperone. Probably in no other play is this fact more clearly revealed. The difference seems to lie rather in a state of mind than in the supposition that the young French men and women *need* a chaperone. The tragedy of the French viewpoint of marriage lies in the fact that whether or not the girl loves the man her family has chosen for her, she must marry him. It is a business deal in Howard's play and nothing else. Of course, the girl's life is ruined until the marriage is found to be illegal.

Howard's *Aristocracy* (1892), is not only an international contrast but a national one, for he has placed side by side a new rich family from California and an old New York family, as well as a group of European patricians. The Laurence family of New York presents a rather exaggerated picture except that Mrs. Laurence's consistent references to the fact that she belongs to the Ten Broecks (the Van Kortlandt branch of the family) is quite in keeping with her type. Otherwise, this particular group of characters seems very unreal and we have no interest in them whatever. Equally uninteresting are the Europeans for they are painted in such an unfavorable light that their unpleasant characters are a source of annoyance. While many old families may go to seed, one gets the impression from this play that patrician is synonymous with immoral.

The Stocktons from California are the only real and lifelike characters in the play. They uphold the tradition of the West in judging a man by what he can *do* rather than by what he knows or by the number of generations he can point out in the family history. Unlike the new rich Americans in Mrs. Bateman's *Golden Calf,* the Stocktons are not crude or vulgar. The scenes of the play are laid in California, London and New York so that we get a touch of the atmosphere of each group with which Howard deals.

Kate, published in 1905, in a form half way between the novel and the drama, as we have noted before, was never produced, but it is one of Howard's finest plays. In this social comedy the scene is laid first in England and then in New York. There is unusually fine character study, especially in the heroine, Kate Hardenbeck, a wealthy American girl; Earl Catherst, her fiance, and Lord John Vernor, a rector whom she loves. Although satire is not Howard's main object, he does satirize the marriage of convenience when an American girl obtains a title, her fiancé's family a fortune. He reveals sympathetically the feelings of the two people involved who do not love each other but who are doing what their families have dictated. Because they admire and respect each other there is a fine understanding between them. The conference between the fathers who cannot agree upon the sum of money that is the basis for the marriage are both amusing and bitterly ironic when one realizes that their children mean little more to them than goods and chattels. *Kate* shows a deeper character study than occurs in Howard's other comedies, with the possible exception of *Young Mrs. Winthrop,* for the sense of breaking down standards which are fundamental to the preservation of essential decency is very clear in the characters of Kate and Earl Catherst.

Clyde Fitch's *Her Great Match,* produced in 1905, is an unusually fine international contrast which shows that Fitch understood European customs as well as those of his own country. The scene is laid in England where we first glimpse a garden fête and later moves to the Botes's home in London. Jo Sheldon and her mother are guests of the Botes's and to the garden fête come Her Royal Highness, Grand Duchess of Hohenstein and her grandson,

H. R. H. Crown Prince Adolph of Eastphalia. Of course, Jo and the Crown Prince fall in love, but they cannot marry unless he gives up his claim to the throne or she consents to a morganatic marriage. The refusal of Jo to accept the latter condition is only natural but Fitch presents the whole problem with rare understanding. Jo Sheldon, like the American girls in Howard's plays, is an example of a frank, sincere and cultured American girl who mingles with perfect assurance and poise with the English and with the royal family of German ancestry. This is one of the merits in Fitch's work which makes him so important a figure in American drama. He had no inferiority complex about being an American and happily he never instills one into any of his characters. Succeeding playwrights followed his example for we cease witnessing the spectacle of either blatant Americans forcing their way around, or of others who are overcome with awkwardness. In like manner, Fitch did not make caricatures of characters beyond the seas. With one exception the English people and the Germans in *Her Great Match* are charming and natural, and what is still more to the point, convincing. Both Jo Sheldon and the Prince win our sympathy and admiration because of their understanding of each other's position.

In the early years of the twentieth century, two playwrights introduced Englishmen into a group of people whose conduct and conversation causes them extreme confusion. *The Earl of Pawtucket* by Augustus Thomas, produced in 1903, centers around an Englishman who tries to pass for an American in order to win the girl he loves. His determination to use American phrases which, of course, he confuses at times, affords some of the most amusing lines in the play. However, Thomas has presented us with a gentleman, a little stupid, perhaps, but one who adheres strictly to his code of honor and who is shocked at times by the free manner of American girls. In many ways, he resembles Sir Wilfrid Cates-Darby in Langdon Mitchell's *New York Idea* (1906), who cannot, to save his life, keep up with the lightning changes in American marriages. When Sir Wilfrid has found out just what the status of each character is, that is, who is married to whom, or who is divorced from whom, he shows considerable ability in keeping pace with the hectic but diverting life around him. He, too, is not a caricature but a very honest portrayal of a very definite type of Englishman with that air of seeming stupidity which is really owing to the English not being able to follow the startling pace set by certain social groups in this country. The fine sense of sportsmanship typical of an Englishman like Cates-Darby is very well brought out in his character.

So This is London, by Arthur Goodrich, produced first at the Hudson Theatre, 1922, is an international contrast between America and England but one which does not present two families of the same class socially. The English family is secure, quiet, reserved, while the American one is an example of the unpolished, new rich element. When the English girl and American boy decide to marry, their respective families are aghast, each father representing in a fade-out scene just what the other people will be like. These two scenes are the best in the play, exaggerated, of course, and yet just about the idea each man would have of the other and his family. When Elinor Beauchamp, the English girl, shows her family a snapshot of the Drapers, her father, Sir Percy, inquires:

> "Who are these creatures?"
> Elinor: "They're Americans, Father, real Americans."
> Lady Beauchamp: "Indians?"

Sir Percy prides himself upon knowing absolutely nothing about America or Americans except that members of the Chamber of Commerce from Rhode Island made a spectacle of themselves in London.

The Drapers, one regrets to say, are addicted to practical joking and revel in baffling the English with what they consider real humor. Essentially, however, they are likeable, and are sincere.

Lady Ducksworth, the most charming character in the play, is a bridge not only between the two families, but also between America and England. American born, she has become an English subject through her marriage, so argues ably in behalf of both sides of the water. It is here that one sees the different treatment afforded another nation from that in the earliest social comedy, *The Contrast.* The effect of the play upon the stage was farcical but it is farce of a high order and there is in many instances the tone of social comedy, while the dialogue is bright and witty.

A play in which the action descends into farce but which seems quite pertinent to the present time is A. E. Thomas's *Just Suppose* (1923), in which the Prince of Wales falls in love with an American girl, Linda Lee Stafford, and comes to her home in the South. The scene between the Prime Minister and Linda is farce, but when one thinks of what can and does happen, he can but remember that "Coming events cast their shadows before."

As Husbands Go, by Rachel Crothers, produced at the John Golden Theatre, New York, March 5th, 1931, is a fine contrast between true and false values and a delightful satire upon women who go abroad and return with their heads turned.

Emmie Sykes, a widow, and Lucile Lingard, wife of Charles Lingard, an unusually fine man whom Lucile has never appreciated, are in Europe when the play opens. Ronald Derbyshire, an English author, has fallen in love with Lucile and she thinks she has fallen in love with him.

> Lucile: ——"I actually don't know what's right and what's wrong. I honestly wish I'd never seen you *at all,* Ronnie. *What am I going to do?"*
> Ronnie: "The greatest *wrong* we can do is to turn our backs on life. If we don't take it full tide as it comes to us—we're rotten little quitters."

Ronnie wishes Lucile to face the situation honestly, tell her husband that she is going to divorce him and then he, Ronnie, will come to America for her. Because of the inherent weakness in her character she is never able to do this. When the two women first get home they try to describe the difference between America and Europe, and here Miss Crothers shows how perfectly ridiculous people generally are when they have let themselves be flattered into thinking they amount to much more than they really do. Also, the unfortunate idea on the part of some Americans that Europe is where they belong is shown for what it is. Lucile and Emmie are telling Emmie's daughter, Peggy, about their trip.

> Lucile: "It was unusual—rather brilliant in fact. I *felt* Europe as I never have before."

> Emmie: "So did I."
> Peggy: "How did it feel?"
> Lucile: "The things that are—interesting and stimulating—and satisfying are *there*. It's all so effortless —so simple. Not strained and made self-conscious as it is over here—it just is."
> Peggy: "*What* is?"
> Emmie: "That's just it. You can't put your finger on it. The air is full of it."
> Lucile: "It isn't something you go *out* for. It's life itself—over there."
> Emmie: "Absolutely. It just oozes out—and you breathe it in."

Charles Lingard's fine character shines through the whole play, especially in his conversation with Hippolitus Lomi, whom Emmie has brought home with her.

> Charles: "It's the experience of a man's soul that makes a country for him."
> Hippie: "It is the experience of a man's soul that makes everything for him—is it not?"
> Charles: "And if a man sees purple mists in his own back-yard—need he travel into the unknown for his soul's sake?"

It is here and in Ronnie's farewell note to Lucile after he has come to America for her but realizes when he meets Charles that it is he who has made Lucile seem perfect, that Miss Crothers brings out the strength and fineness of character without which there could be no worthwhile basis for society. The last lines of Ronnie's note to Lucile bring into sharp contrast her character and that of her husband.

> "I have seen the magnificent simplicity of a big man —the shining glory of a selfless love that has enveloped you and made you perfect in its own beauty."

What stands out particularly in the work of Rachel Crothers is her keen interest in life, and her ability to present it not only faithfully but always in an entertaining and intelligent way. Her character creations are nearly always of a high order so that one does not forget them, while her dialogue is natural and generally sparkles with a ready wit and lively repartee. Never do her characters lose their sense of values but they are always aware of them and are guided by them. With a fine sense of balance she never lets either her humorous characters become dull through saying too much, or the serious discussions of the main problem become tiresome or heavy. What is more to the point, she frequently endows some of her most amusing people with the soundest philosophy of all but she has them express it in what seems a scatter-brained, even ridiculous manner. She knows that people remember longer something that has made them laugh—even though it be an unpleasant truth—than they do a serious or dull expression of that truth.

The last play in which either the major portion of the action or all of it occurs in a country other than America is S. N. Behrman's *Rain from Heaven* (1935). Of plot there is little for the play is rather an interchange of opinions upon present day conditions. It deals with the question of dictatorship, of League of Youth Movements and touches on Communism. It shows how conversation in the drawing room has ceased to be mere idle gossip or just clever talk for its own sake. More and more is it becoming tinged with the national problems that are growing more pressing every day. The scene of *Rain from Heaven* is laid in the charming living room of Lady Wyngate's home, not far from London. Lady Wyngate backs a very liberal paper, houses refugees from unsympathetic governments and is at dagger points with conservative capitalists who accuse her wrongly of being a Communist. What really stands out in her character is goodness of heart and an intense dislike of injustice.

> "I hate dictatorship because it implies omniscience and
> I don't believe in omniscience. That's theology applied
> to politics, and I believe it's dangerous. I can believe in
> God only if He's invisible."

Hugo Willens is a German refugee. Because he wrote an article entitled "The Last Jew," a satire, he was clapped into a concentration camp for a while. Someone discovered that his great grandmother was a Jewess and Hugo is now an exile from his country. Lael Wyngate feels that he is too bitter over his personal misfortune.

> Lael: ——"but aren't you mistaking a mass antagonism for a personal one? Hugo, you don't want to develop a persecution mania."
> Hugo: "Is it a mania for the persecuted to believe in the reality of persecution?"
> Lael: "No. The truth is there's a pest over all the world just now, an epidemic of hatred and intolerance that may engulf us all. That is perfectly possible. People have suffered too much during the last twenty years—they can't stand any more, that's all—"

There are, of course, many lighter moments in the play. For example, Lady Wyngate has taken her guests to see the moving picture, "The House of Rothschild," but unfortunately some of them left before it was over, which upsets Lady Wyngate.

> Hugo: "Did Lord Rothschild go to heaven?"
> Lael: "He did and in color, my dear, in color! Suddenly and with divine unreasonableness, Lord Rothschild and everybody else became iridescent."
> (Everyone laughs.)
> "He went to a big ball in the palace to be slapped on the back by the King. Good old Rothschild lends money to the Allies for patriotism and four per cent. You could see his pearl shirt-studs glisten with pride —you simply must come with me to see the end of that picture."

The Americans in the play, two brothers, represent the capitalistic viewpoint. The younger of the two, a famous aviator, loves Lael Wyngate but, because neither can ever actually understand the other due to the difference in their fundamental viewpoints, they separate. The elder brother, a rather pig-headed individual, is irksome in his intolerance and his inability to follow more than one line of thought, but he is, without a doubt, a very real character whom one meets in public life.

The play is a search for justice, for human goodness, which are being stifled today. Behrman might have written a social drama dealing with politics, mass movements and their like, but he has chosen, happily, to make the drawing room of an intellectual woman of breeding the scene for his play and to fill this room with highly intelligent, civilized people who represent the various conflicting interests of today, and who can discuss these interests in a manner that is most appealing.

One value of plays which deal with an international contrast lies in the revelation of the social standards of the different countries. The American comedies which we have just considered vary widely in the treatment both of foreign characters and of foreign standards. We have seen how it was the custom in the early plays to satirize and caricature Europeans and European manners. In the middle nineteenth century we witnessed new rich Americans trying to gain titles through marriage with European nobility. The later drama satirizes neither new rich Americans nor Europeans but presents pictures of characters who belong to the same social class and who mingle in a perfectly natural way together.

Bronson Howard's social comedies of international contrast, *One of Our Girls* and *Kate* were among the first to make a study of the different viewpoints held by American and European society. Particularly is this true of *One of Our Girls,* which penetrates far beneath superficial appearances. Like Fitch's *Her Great Match* the Continental outlook upon marriage is brought to light. Both dramatists show complete understanding of the essential laws upon which Continental society is founded. In Fitch's play we feel more sympathetic toward the Germans than we do toward the French in Howard's, but this is due to the different times in which the plays are laid and to the plots.

With *Rain from Heaven,* the last play discussed under this particular phase, there is little thought of an actual international contrast. It is true that the political conditions in England, Germany and America come under consideration, but the characters themselves mingle together with such ease that one forgets the difference in their nationalities, the interest centering mainly in personalities and what the characters have to say. In the light of this play, there is evident a steady trend away from the attempt to satirize or caricature characters from other countries. The contrast is becoming less apparent.

B. THE SOCIAL SCENE OF THE PAST

Probably one of the most difficult tasks for a playwright to accomplish is to transfer successfully the atmosphere of a past age to contemporary times.   There have been numberless attempts to do this with varying degrees of success.   A play based upon historical facts is simpler to present than is one in which the playwright must try to portray the social life of a bygone day for, generally speaking, he must invent a great deal and transmit a certain intangible quality to the realm of reality.   Unless the play rings with an authentic note it cannot succeed, but remains an artificial picture in which we cannot believe.   A happy collaboration gave to American literature an outstanding success in this particular field of drama.

Charles the Second, produced at the Park Theatre, New York, 1826, was adapted from *"La Jeunesse de Henri V"* by Alexandre Duval, which in turn was based upon *Charles II, roi d'Angleterre en un certain lieu,* by Sébastien Mercier.   In this play John Howard Payne and Washington Irving have caught not only the true spirit of high comedy but have captured and reproduced faithfully the atmosphere of a former day.   The plot centers around the reformation of Charles II through a trick on the part of the Earl of Rochester, the Queen and Lady Clara.   There is excellent character drawing; the dialogue is rapid and sparkling, while the situations are handled with such deftness that they do not become farcical.   This very fact is proof of the authors' complete understanding of social values.   The gay, carefree atmosphere of the court of Charles II flashes before us with its spirit of fun and adventure but never for a moment does one of the characters lose either his or her innate sense of fundamental social values.   Payne and Irving have reconstructed vividly a lively chapter in England's history.   When, at the end of the play, Charles II discovers the trick that his friends have played upon him, his sense of honor and essential decency that make him a gentleman prevent him from behaving in a manner unbecoming to his position.   It is the recognition on the part of all the characters of the necessity for upholding certain standards, that raises the play to the high level it maintains.

The play follows Duval's closely as to plot and the names of the leading characters are the same except for Mary Copp who is "Betty" in the French. Duval had to change his hero from Charles II to Henry V because the French censor was afraid that the audiences would think of "the Cromwell who then governed France."[2] There is a scene in the English play which takes place outside of Captain Copp's tavern that is not in Duval's play, and of course, Captain Copp's song which he never manages to finish is a delightful touch very likely written by Irving. All of the songs in *Charles II* are original and there are frequent changes in the dialogue. However, the situations and action are very similar while the same spirit of high comedy pervades both plays. Payne's and Irving's play seems to have a dash and sparkle that the French version cannot quite match and the atmosphere is English.

In 1852, George Henry Boker's social comedy, *The Widow's Marriage* was produced. It is a blank verse play laid in London in the time of George II. Lady Goldstraw, a widow, is besieged by young suitors who wish to marry her for her money. A very vain and foolish woman, she listens rapturously to the nonsense which these young men speak. Her frantic attempts to try to remain young are a source of frequent amusement throughout the play. Finally, by means of a trick played upon her, she sees how ridiculous she is and ceases to try to keep her daughter, Madge, in the background. In this play Boker has caught the spirit of the times accurately. The characters, especially Lady Goldstraw and Lord Ruffler to whom she thinks she's married, are very real. Despite the spectacle that she has made of herself we cannot help feeling sorry for the widow during the trial she endures. However, the crowning triumph of the play is when she admits that she is sixty-three!

A gay and carefree spirit pervades this comedy; the atmosphere of an age that was none too scrupulous or particular. Very well indeed has Boker depicted at least one side of the social life of a past age in England. The fact that he has chosen blank

---

[2] Quinn, *A History of the American Drama from the Beginning to the Civil War,* p. 180.

verse gives to the play a certain tone which it very likely would not have had if he had written it in prose. When we turn now to a play with America as its scene we find a sure sense of values and an accurate picture of the past.

Love in '76, by Oliver Bell Bunce, was produced at Laura Keene's Theatre, New York, 1857. As the title indicates, the action takes place during the Revolutionary War in 1776. The plot centers around Rose Elsworth and Captain Walter Armstrong, who are in love with each other. Captain Armstrong is in the Colonial Army while Harry Elsworth, Rose's brother, is in the British Army for both he and his father are Tories. Armstrong is being held a prisoner in the Elsworth home, for a British detachment under Major Cleveland has arrived. Major Cleveland has promised Rose not to harm Captain Armstrong but in order that she shall never be able to marry him, the Major plans to trick Armstrong into a marriage with Bridget, the maid. Of course, Rose fools him and pretends to be the maid. When the Major tries to break his word, Rose announces that she will publicly disgrace him. This she knows she can do because the strength of the social code of the British army holds Cleveland to his promise. The very existence of a parole system was based on the assumption that an officer would not break his word. Regardless of the subterfuge to which Rose has had to resort, she never for a moment loses the qualities of the gentlewoman that she is and this serves all the better to heighten the contrast between her and Major Cleveland. He lacks any sense of decency; is a cad who descends to the lowest trick possible to gain a small revenge.

A very clear picture of how families were divided in their allegiance to the two causes in the Revolution occurs when Rose Elsworth and her father are discussing Walter Armstrong's being made a captain.

> Elsworth: "Not a rebel, I trust."
> Rose: "Not a traitor, I thank Heaven."
> Elsworth: "You confound terms strangely. A traitor is one false to his king."
> Rose: "False to his country, sir. A king is a creature of today—your country a thing of immortality."

Elsworth: "Your king is your sovereign, by divine right
and true succession."
Rose: "Then, sir, serve the Stuarts. How came the house
of Hanover upon the throne? You see, sir, that
if you zealous loyalists could shift off James, we,
with less belief in the divine right of kings, can shift
off George."

Needless to say, by the time Major Cleveland has displayed his
black soul, the Elsworth family has no objections to Rose's marriage with Captain Armstrong, but all through the play we are
aware of the tragedy that a war brings to families and friends
when some of them are loyal to one side and others to the opposing force. This same theme ran through several of the Civil
War plays, *Barbara Frietchie* being one of them. Before taking
up this play of Clyde Fitch, we shall consider another one of his
which takes us to England again.

Beau Brummell was written especially for Richard Mansfield
,and produced by him at the Madison Square Theatre, New York,
in 1890. A romantic comedy of manners, *Beau Brummell* is
based upon the life of George Brummell, a Georgian dandy. Fitch
has reproduced with notable success another age, for among his
many other endowments was his ability to grasp the atmosphere of
another nation and time and to recognize its social codes. The
artificial customs of the Georgian period are clear in this play.
Complete control of the emotions (evidenced in Beau's insistence
upon "a glance of the eye" rather than a hearty hand shake as
a greeting) is one of the social artificialities that existed. Another
was the disgrace of being addressed by an inferior when strolling
in the Mall. Equally important at this time was the meticulous
mode of dress. Society in this age resembled that of the Restora-
tion period in its emphasis upon a polished surface while it winked
at what was going on behind the scenes. That morals counted for
very little is evident in *Beau Brummell*, but equally evident is
the recognition on the part of the characters of the standards
which, to all appearances, society must maintain.

Beau Brummell is a man who lives entirely for himself, an
opportunist, and one to whom appearances form an obsession, but
underneath all of this lies a really heroic character. The devotion

of Mortimer, his valet, proves that Beau possesses beneath a superficial exterior, the qualities upon which loyalty and trust may be founded.   At the end of the play we see that Mortimer's unswerving loyalty has not gone amiss, for Beau's sacrifice squares with his ideal in life.   The play gives an almost perfect picture of an individual who possesses great strength of character beneath what seems a shallow exterior and at the same time of one whose obsession amounts to eccentricity.   Regardless of what is occurring either to him or around him, Beau never for a moment will show a trace of emotion, for this would not be in keeping with his ideal of the gentleman.   The apparent lack of any human feeling during this period Fitch has transmitted to his play, but at the same time he has raised the curtain occasionally to give us a glimpse into the real characters of these people.   *Beau Brummell* is an excellent example of the social scene of the past.

In 1899 *Barbara Frietchie,* based upon Whittier's poem, but with little consideration for historical fact, was produced.   The play is a tragedy but the first act is social comedy, for in it we witness the pleasant life in an old Southern town.   The light, happy conversation of the sons and daughters of families who have been intimate for generations establishes a quiet atmosphere of an unruffled social life which forms a striking contrast to the tragic ending.   Again Fitch has caught the atmosphere of another day and age and has managed to transport us into another environment.

The social scene of the past is always interesting from an historical point of view.   When the manners and customs of a past age are presented in dramatic form there is a note of reality that does not appear in other forms of literature.   In *Charles the Second,* for instance, we seem to live with the characters and to share with them the spirit of their day.   The social standards during the reign of the "Merry Monarch" come to light in this play because both Payne and Irving were men who were in a position to understand them and to translate them into their play.   The English scenes of both *Charles the Second* and of Fitch's *Beau Brummell* have an authentic note, for the playwrights in each case were not only fitted to portray manners, but were interested in the historical background as well.   Unfortunately, *His Grace de Grammont* of

Clyde Fitch was not available at the time of this survey of social comedy. It is laid in the time of Charles II.

Oliver Bell Bunce's *Love in '76* shows an equally sure knowledge of social laws and an understanding of the age in which the play is laid. The strict social code of the army upon which much of the action depends is very clearly brought out by Bunce. To break this code spells not only social ostracism but complete disgrace. Rose Elsworth, the heroine, knows this and holds Major Cleveland to his promise on the strength of this knowledge.

These three plays are good pictures of the times with which they deal, and they show a sure understanding of the social laws which motivate the actions of the characters. Boker's play *The Widow's Marriage,* while interesting in certain respects, does not give us the same sense of reality. It has some very amusing scenes and the characters are well drawn but we miss the vivid impression of another period in history that we get from *Charles the Second, Love in '76* and *Beau Brummell.*

C.   THE CONFLICT BETWEEN SOCIETY AND THE INDIVIDUAL

Society as a whole is always on guard against the individual, ready to crush individual expression that may in any way deviate from the set standards by which we live, and unless the individual is strong enough to rise above his environment and throw off the shackles that chain him to the monotony of every day life he will remain an unidentified member of the herd. This struggle between society and the individual has been going on since the world began, but in recent years it has become more violent because of the changing standards that the turmoil of modern civilization has brought about. Loud and long was the crash of many conventions after the World War, and for a time, chaos reigned. Many persons, it is true, never changed one iota but continued to remain immobile and clung to the same principles they had always cherished. Sometimes we find that the struggle between society and the individual arises not from any changing standards owing to wars or industrial revolutions but to certain traits in the individuals themselves.

Several playwrights have taken up the study of a particular weakness in a human being's character which makes it difficult for that individual to uphold his or her place in society. Augustus Thomas, Clyde Fitch and A. E. Thomas are three outstanding American dramatists who have written plays which center around persons of this kind. Two of Clyde Fitch's finest plays, *The Girl with the Green Eyes* (1902), and *The Truth* (1906), are studies of individuals whose inherent weakness nearly wrecks their lives as well as their homes.

The Girl with the Green Eyes is a study of jealousy. Jinny Austin has inherited from her parents a tendency toward an almost insane jealousy. This is shown particularly well in the first scene when Jinny and her husband, John Austin, are ready to start on their wedding trip. What finally wrecks the happiness of Jinny and John Austin is that Jinny's brother, Geoffrey, whom she adores, is a bigamist. He has secretly married a housemaid and then marries Ruth Chester, one of Jinny's best friends. Both Ruth and Geoffrey have taken John Austin into their confidence but he tries to keep the matter hidden from Jinny. However, blinded by jealousy, she refuses to trust her husband and accuses him of having an affair with Ruth. At last he leaves her, after he and Ruth have told her about Geoffrey, and Jinny attempts suicide but John and her father return in time to save her.

Primarily, the play is a domestic drama but it is shot through with some excellent social contrasts. The second scene, which opens in the Vatican, is a priceless picture of the ignorant, sheeplike tourists who wander past Jinny while she is waiting for her husband. Half-dead, but determined, they pursue their sightseeing, losing their way in the labyrinth of rooms, making constant inquiry as to their whereabouts and finally giving vent to their miserable state with scathing remarks upon the art which they have worn themselves to the bone to see. A Mrs. Lopp and her daughter, Carrie, pause near Jinny Austin for a few moments, the following conversation took place:

> Mrs. Lopp: "What's this, Carrie?"
> Carrie (Looking in her Baedeker): "I don't know; I've sort of lost my place, somehow!"
> Mrs. Lopp: "Well, we must be in Room No. 3 or 4—ain't we?"
> Carrie: (Reads out): "The big statue at the end of Room No. 3 is Diana the Huntress."

Mrs. Lopp: "This must be it, then,—Diana! Strong-looking woman, ain't she?"

Carrie: "Yes, very nice. You know she was the goddess who wouldn't let the men see her bathe."

Mrs. Lopp: "Mercy, Carrie! and did all the other goddesses? I don't think much of their habits. I suppose this is the same person those Italians sell on the streets at home, and call the Bather."

(Jinny is secretly very much amused. Finally she speaks.)

Jinny: "Excuse me, but you are in one of the cabinets— and this is the Apollo Belvedere."

The whole scene is almost incomparable and affords comic relief to an otherwise serious drama, but at the same time it is a preparation for the meeting between Jinny and the Cullinghams, who have brought Ruth Chester to Europe with them, which at once arouses Jinny's suspicions. The gradual and natural way in which Fitch shows how the sparks of jealousy in Jinny are fanned into flames is proof of his knowledge of human nature. However, not only is this penetrating study of a person's character of absorbing interest but we are always aware of the social background, of the actions on the part of the people around Jinny which contribute to the undermining of her character.

When we turn to the next play in which Clyde Fitch selected an individual with an inherent weakness, we are all the more conscious of society's part in building up this weakness. In *The Truth* the playwright presents a vivid picture of the so-called necessary prevarications which society feels itself called upon to make. Becky Warder, the central figure, cannot tell the truth, and finally as each lie leads to another and more serious one, she nearly destroys her marriage. As indicated, this weakness in her is fed constantly by society, which avoids the truth whenever possible. The constant social intrigues, the habit of being "not at home," polite flattery, all make Becky feel that her continual practice of avoiding the truth is perfectly in keeping with the life around her. This is one of the important points that Fitch emphasizes—the effect of certain accepted habits or customs upon an individual who is unable to distinguish between the right and the wrong time to make use of them. Becky Warder is a more sympathetic character than Jinny Austin for many times her prevaricating arises because of her generosity. For instance, she has promised her husband that she will not send more money to her father, a gentleman who has fallen considerably in the social scale owing to his gambling. However, upon one pretext or another she obtains the money from her husband and sends it to her father, and since we know that she is doing it because she loves him and is sorry for him, we feel sympathetic toward her. Although her flirting is a more serious fault and her lies to her husband on this score are more worthy of condemnation, Fitch shows that Becky is so perfectly sure of her love for her husband that she feels she is doing nothing wrong. Besides, this is another little habit that most of her friends have, so why not she?

The fact that in both of these plays Fitch has drawn the characters of the husbands in direct contrast to their wives heightens the effect considerably. John Austin is without a trace of jealousy; Tom Warder is a person who would never consider anything but truth and frankness. And, to finish the picture, we have the background of society with all the forces that either contribute to destroying an individual or add to his strength of character if he can rise above them.

In 1905 Augustus Thomas's *Mrs. Leffingwell's Boots* provided a psychological study of a man who, because of a blow upon his head years before, is dishonest. He is not a kleptomaniac but is an individual in whom all sense of honor is gone. The friend who was accidentally the cause of the blow protects him despite the fact that the friend in consequence becomes estranged from the girl whom he loves. The dinner party to which everyone involved comes, turns out to be a complete failure, for the worst blizzard "since Roscoe Conklin died" sets in, and most of the guests cannot leave their homes. However, either by chance or because a few have braved the storm, there are enough to make a small party and the final unravelling of the plot is good theatre. The play is primarily a psychological study but it may still be classed as social comedy because of the function which brings the characters together and because of the obviously secure position the characters occupy. Thomas shows very well the way in which one person, through malice, may cause what, to all appearances, is a scandal.

Society is never prone to believe anything except what it sees and if appearances are bad, the matter is settled. This dearth of faith on the part of society Thomas brings out very well, showing how everyone is ready to believe the worst.

In 1910, A. E. Thomas's *Her Husband's Wife,* presented us with a study of a very different kind of person but one who, unfortunately, is ever present in life. It is one of the most laugh provoking and yet thought provoking comedies of its time. Laid against the fast life of the racing season at Saratoga, is the story of Irene Randolph, a hypochondriac, who is convinced that she is going to die and has picked out her husband's second wife for him. The play reflects one of those constantly recurring vogues for doctoring since a friend of Irene's is said to have six doctors and an osteopath. Although some of the situations become farcical, the character of Irene keeps the play from descending into real farce, while both the dialogue and atmosphere of the play belong to social comedy. Ridiculous as Irene appears to be when she is trying to decide between her red and green medicine at certain hours, her case is actually pathetic, even tragic, and Thomas manages to present this aspect as well as the humorous one. This poking fun at a foolish and, in this instance, a dangerous popular whim is, of course, one of the chief functions of social comedy. Thomas may have used Daly's *Love in Tandem* as a source for his play since Daly also shows a woman who is picking out a second wife for her husband. However, in that case the woman is not ill but just tired of her husband and the play does not have a serious motive.

Probably one of the most amusing and ironic plays we have which deals with the conflict between society and the individual is Percy Mackaye's *Anti-Matrimony* (1910). In this instance we witness two young people who have been married in Europe but who have vowed to conceal the fact in order to carry on the modern crusade for complete freedom. "Freedom is the first thing, and freedom is based in the individual; but the home undermines the individual, converting him to a tyrant or a slave. Therefore the first act of a free community must be to abolish the home." This is the professed ideal of the young husband. His wife extols in glowing terms to her sister the shining example set by Rebecca West.

> "*She* was not the dupe of matrimonial ghosts. She shocked the world and taught her lover to shock it. To-gether they obeyed the call of their super-souls, and she leaned on her lover's heart as they went forth to the mill-race." (Melodramatically) "O my Mildred, must I also be driven to the dark waters?"

The way in which these two young people are finally forced to acknowledge their marriage affords some of the most hilarious comedy in American drama. The satire and irony are devastating but never bitter. The play affords an excellent example of social comedy as a cure for a dangerous movement which threatened some of the essential laws of society.

In 1915 a play with two distinct themes, either one of which would have made a complete drama, but neither of which, as the case stands, is fully developed, was produced at the 39th Street Theatre, New York, on October the 9th. *The Unchastened Woman,* by Louis Kaufman Anspacher, is a splendid study, so far as it goes, of a completely cold, unmoral woman whose sole amusement is to lead men on to a certain point and when they have fallen in love with her, turn without ado to someone else. Caroline Knollys refuses to divorce her husband, Herbert, because she enjoys the protection his name gives her. They lead totally separate lives but never once has she overstepped her bounds. She remains chaste physically, but in every other way has smashed conventions and is totally devoid of any ethical code. The play just misses being a masterly psychological study of a very definite type of woman.

The other theme which is partially developed is the clash be-tween capital and labor. This is introduced plausibly enough, for Caroline is at present interested in an artist whose wife has de-voted her life to helping the working classes. Michael Krellin, a labor agitator, is the mouthpiece for the masses and the argu-ments between him and Caroline sum up neatly the standpoint of the two opposing groups. Caroline, he points out, belongs to the class whose fortunes are made in industry protected by the govern-ment, but to a class which is most eager to evade the customs imposed by that government to protect the industries. Indeed, in the opening scene of the play Caroline has just arrived from

Europe and rather than pay customs duty which will entail being annoyed, she evades the customs, preferring to be fined.

The study of social and industrial problems has become more and more widespread so that it confronts us at every turn. The theatre itself is reflecting constantly this unrest for there are playwrights whose dramas are based solely upon labor problems. However, long discussions which deal with the rights of capital and labor are not dramatic and the whole subject is one which is far better suited to debates, newspapers, magazines and books devoted to the topic. Nevertheless, the fact remains that the stage is taking up the question to a greater extent than ever before and so Anspacher's play is particularly interesting when one realizes how it pointed forward to the present day. The trouble with the play is that the combination of social comedy and industrial unrest is not a happy one, for neither theme in this particular instance is fully developed because both require a full, and not a partial, treatment. To begin with, social comedy does not deal with the laboring classes but with a distinctly different element in society. The very definition of social comedy excludes at once the masses so that to try to bring into one play two themes dealing with totally different classes in society is a practically impossible feat.

One of the most delightful writers of gay, glittering comedy is Clare Kummer, whose ability to create interesting situations out of thin air and characters who literally float through life, stamps her with an individuality all her own. The spirit and dialogue never fail while beneath all the surface froth, her work is shot through with keen, playful satire. *Good Gracious, Annabelle,* produced at the Republic Theatre, New York, on October 31st, 1916, is called a romantic farce but both the tone of the play and the characterization raise it above farce while the clever, and often brilliant, dialogue belongs to the comedy of manners. Mrs. Kummer has a deftness and lightness of touch that very few writers possess. None of the characters in *Good Gracious, Annabelle* actually has any sense of responsibility toward life. They simply accept what comes along with a charming naïveté, never for a moment actually concerned. Annabelle manages to guide not only her own, but the destinies of her friends, through several trying situations, for whatever serious side of her nature may be lacking, she is richly endowed with feminine intuition which seldom fails her. Her very sureness of social laws aids her in the extremity in which she finds herself and she emerges triumphant over all obstacles. This is a case in which an individual rises serenely above any difficulties that may beset her path.

Rollo's Wild Oat, on the other hand, shows how social convention hampers an individual so that he cannot rise out of the groove in which he has always lived. This play, produced in 1920, has some devastating satire on the wealthy, snobbish young man who insists upon becoming an actor. Always conscious that he is superior socially to the people around him, and filled with extraordinary ego, he is, of course, hopeless as an actor. The calamity that befalls his production of "Hamlet," and the subsequent scenes in the house of his grandfather, who has commanded him to come home, are shot through with irony, but are so full of genuine good humor that there is no trace of bitterness.

In 1924 Rachel Crothers' *Expressing Willie* satirized the cult of self-expression. Willie Smith has made a fortune in toothpaste and has built a ridiculously large and pseudo-artistic house on Long Island. About him are gathered a group of sophisticated people who, though thinking him a laughing stock, flatter him. Frances Sylvester, who poses as a disciple of freedom—"Complete and utter expression of one's self," as she puts it—is one of those intolerable hypocrites who veils her natural instincts in affected talk comprehensible to no one. After Willie's mother, who is never fooled by appearances, inquires what went on in Willie's room the night before, Frances tells her she must be a bit of a mystic.

> Frances: "You seem to be very psychic—so sensitive to conditions."
> Mrs. Smith: "I have very good hearing and eyesight—if that's what you mean."

Meanwhile, Minnie, a plain, simple soul whom Willie's mother hopes he will marry, explains her presence in Willie's room the night before, sending the other guests into gales of laughter, except Frances, who remarks:

> "It hurts me to see the rest of you so horribly material. It shows me you might even misinterpret what *I* did."

Taliaferro, an artist, wishes to bring out Minnie's musical ability. In a tilt with Mrs. Smith while discussing suppressions, which he believes no one should have, Mrs. Smith replies:

> "I'm not so sure about that. If we were all running around without any *suppressions,* we might as well have tails again."
> Taliaferro: "I don't get a sense of much suppression on your part, dear lady."
> Mrs. Smith: "You don't! Well, I'm suppressing more this minute than most people feel in a life time. If I was to let go now—God help Willie."

In the end, Willie's expression comes out when he realizes he loves Minnie—once again an example of Miss Crothers' faith in human beings, believing that in the final analysis what is best in us will come to the top. The contrast between the different characters is very striking. Each is representative of a certain phase of life but in no way is anyone just a type. They are all very real people whom one might easily encounter at a week-end house party.

Philip Barry's *In a Garden* (1925), is the study of a woman who refuses to believe that life must follow a certain pattern and that everything can be scientifically explained. Lissa Terry lives in an imaginative world of her own and cannot view life with the appraising eye that her husband, Adrian, does. He is a playwright who cannot hear a phrase or see a situation without thinking of its dramatic effect. He even regards Lissa as a character in a play and not as an actual human being. In speaking of life, Adrian says:

> "It's simplicity itself. First, look on life always with an artist's eye, get an angle—an *angle*—and keep it. Then take the everyday material as any fine artist does—and arrange—select—condense—"
> Lissa: "I'm sorry, but I'm afraid that for me, life's got to be taken whole. I can't imagine it otherwise. It's—

just the feel of it I love so—the unexpectedness. . . ."

Adrian: "But, my dear—there need be nothing unexpected in this world! You know that!"

Lissa: "No, I don't."

Adrian: "Then it's time you did. Because I assure you,
there's cause and effect wherever you look—a basic
reason for everything."

Lissa: "Why is it birds fly, 'Drian—instead of walking
soberly along the ground?"

Adrian: "Because a pterodactyl once climbed a tree, that's
why."

Lissa: "You're not really going to *tell* me!"

But he *has* told her and again one of the things which she loved
to think of as *not* being planned is scientifically explained and
therefore ruined. "Life lived as high comedy with ourselves as
dramatists and characters, directors, scene-shifters, actors and
audience," is Adrian's idea.

At the end of the play Lissa leaves Adrian for she feels that
she must be free to think things out for herself. Perhaps she
will return to him, perhaps not. We do not know. Most of her
illusions that she held dearest are scattered, and before every one
disappears she must escape from an atmosphere that is stifling
her.

There is a certain atmosphere of fantasy and an imaginative
quality which at times lift the play out of real life into another
sphere. We cannot, of course, live totally in a world of fancy
but without some imagination and without any dreams life is a
dried and shrivelled bargain.

In 1927 S. N. Behrman's *The Second Man* opened at the Guild
Theatre, New York. Before us is the spectacle of a young girl
glorying in the new freedom that has come to her generation, to
her own sex especially, trying to force Clark Storey, an "imitative
poet and second-rate" short story writer to become her lover when
he refuses to marry her. That he doesn't become her lover is
owing partly to an innate sense of decency and partly to the fact
that he knows he will lose the financial assistance of a wealthy
widow who is in love with him. Like the *Second Man,* in Willa
Cather's *Alexander's Bridge,* the two very different sides of Clark

Storey's nature symbolize to a certain extent two phases of life. One is a light, rather charming but superficial side while the other —the Second Man—is a cynical, harsh side, the outgrowth of failure to achieve a goal. Although not an admirable figure by any means, we like Clark Storey for his honesty about himself. Despite the unconventional atmosphere of the play we see the characters reacting against the breaking down of certain social standards. Storey himself will not shatter these creeds, although on the other hand, he is not strong enough to rise above mediocrity because he can always depend upon someone else.

Holiday, by Philip Barry, which opened at the Plymouth Theatre, New York, on November 26th, 1928, is a delightful revelation of the life of the pompous, very wealthy and conservative New Yorker to whom tradition and money mean everything. Edward Seton, in fact, looks upon himself as a tradition, so heavily is he weighed down by his importance. He can't be wrong and no one, except Linda, his younger daughter, ever really opposes his will or admits that the whole Seton tribe may possibly be ridiculous. When Johnny Case falls in love with Julia, Linda's sister, and comes to the house to meet his future father-in-law, Linda assumes her father's air and prepares Johnny for the worst. This immediately gives us the whole background of the Setons. Linda first asks Johnny whether he is a man of means.

> Johnny (rising): "I have in my pocket now thirty-four dollars and a package of Lucky Strikes. Have one?"
> Linda: "Thanks." (She takes cigarette) "But no Gilt-edged Securities? No rolling woodlands?"
> Johnny: "I've got a few shares of Common Stock tucked away in a warm place."
> Linda: "Common? Don't say the word." (She accepts a light from Johnny, and seats herself, sighing) "I'm afraid it won't do Julia—He's a comely boy, but probably just another of the vast army of clock-watchers."
> Ned: (from behind his newspaper) "How are you socially?"
> Johnny: "Nothing there, either."
> Linda: "You mean to say your mother wasn't even a Whoosits?"

When Julia and Ned go to greet their father Linda
mimics the socialites.
Linda: "However do you do, Mr. Case?"
Johnny: "And you, Miss—ah—"
Linda: "Seton is the name."
Johnny: "Not one of the bank Setons?"
Linda: "The same."
Johnny: "Fancy! I hear November cats are up four
points."
Linda: "Have you been to the opera lately?"
Johnny: "Only in fits and starts, I'm afraid."
Linda: "But, my dear—we must do something for them!
They entertained us in Rome."
Johnny: "And you really saw Mt. Everest?"
Linda: "Chit."
Johnny: "Chat."

When Johnny is about ready for his interview with Edward
Seton, Linda exhorts him with the ominous words:

"Go on, Case. Don't expect simplicity here—just
think of our Fifth Avenue frontage."

As the play progresses Johnny reveals his idea of having his
holiday first and working later, an attitude very un-American,
thinks the elder Seton. Linda, siding with Johnny, exclaims:

"Then he's a bad one and will go to hell when he dies.
Because apparently he can't quite believe that a life
devoted to piling up money is all it's cracked up to
be. That's strange, isn't it—when he has us, right
before his eyes, for such a shining example."
Julia: "I thought you were the one who found leisure
so empty."
Linda: "And so it may be for him—yes—maybe it will!
But he's got a right to discover that for himself.
Can't you see that?"

The play deals with two entirely different viewpoints of life.
That of the smug, complacent, conservative person to whom
money and security are everything, and that of the person who
still has imagination, the spirit of adventure that hasn't been killed

by stuffy convention. "At least," the latter cries, "give me the chance." Julia, in siding with her father, acts as social convention has taught her, when she gives up Johnny, while Linda breaks down the barriers when she dashes from the house at the end of the play to join Johnny on his adventure.

Hotel Universe, produced at the Martin Beck Theatre, New York, on April 14th, 1930, is a far more serious play although Barry's light touch in the dialogue carries it swiftly along and provides the keen humor which is an integral part of his work. The play centers around a group of people who belong to what has been ominously termed the "lost generation." The house of Stephen Field and his daughter, Ann, had been a small hotel, Hotel de l'Univers, but it was deserted because strange things happened. "People began to resemble other people and the place itself, other places. And time went sort of funny. Their pasts kept cropping up." Ann's friends, a group of people disillusioned with the crashing of values and standards after the war, are spending the week-end with her. The following discussion reveals the hopeless state of the so-called "lost generation."

> Pat: "And what's the big premium on life, I'd like to know?"
> Norman: "Well, it does look like all we've got."
> Pat: "There was a great big war, Pet, and we survived it. We're living on borrowed time."
> Tom: "Lost! One battalion."
> Pat: "We're not lost. Our schedule is different, that's all. What I mean is, we'll have had the works at forty instead of eighty."
> Norman: "I've got a theory people expect too much from life."
> Ann: "But you can't! That's one thing that's not possible."
> Lily: "Then why is everyone so disappointed in it?"
> Ann: "Because all they concern themselves with are its probabilities. Think of the things that might happen, can happen, do happen! The possibilities!"
>   - - - - - -
>   - - - - - -
> Tom: "A person's got to look for disillusionment all the way along. It's the price paid by everyone who uses his head for anything but a hat-rack."

An atmosphere of the supernatural envelopes the play, for not only does Barry deal with that aspect of life which we see around us every day but he shows that life is made up of three estates; the present, the imaginative, and one beyond these which includes them both. *Hotel Universe* reveals life as a great but grim comedy. It is a powerful play in which we see that every individual must be released from some obsession before he can be happy. There is a struggle in everyone against certain forces which will crush him unless he can find some means for overcoming them. As soon as the characters in *Hotel Universe* have been freed from the obsessions that have warped them they are able to face life once more. There is bitter irony in the play when we realize how individuals are disillusioned and finally defeated by an incident in their lives or a weakness in their characters which they might easily overcome were it not for the constant pressure of society. Some of them escape through suicide, while others take refuge in a bitter cynicism. Whatever illusions the characters in *Hotel Universe* cherished were swept away by the World War so that nothing but a hopeless feeling remained. Their weapons of self-defense against the overwhelming odds that life piled upon them were gone.

The Animal Kingdom (1932) is a study of a rather different standard of society from that found in *Holiday*. In this play we meet two very charming people who are in love with each other but who have broken down one of the most fundamental codes of society. Tom and Daisy have been living together for years without the sanctity of marriage. He is a writer and she an artist and their life together surrounded by a congenial group of people, has been happy and unmolested. When Daisy is in Europe, Tom marries a girl who cares for nothing except his father's money, which will make her a leader. When he realizes that Cecilia is completely selfish, has no real affection for him, and finds that to accomplish what she wants she relies entirely upon her physical allure for him, he despises her. She now wishes to move from the country into town with Tom's father where she can reign in all her glory. Tom's father has sent him a very large check for his birthday which Tom refuses to accept.

Cecilia: "But there isn't that much money in the world."

Tom: "In Father's world, there is. He feels he can afford it to get us to come live with him."

Cecilia: "Of course, I don't understand your attitude about that, either."

Tom: "Don't you, C?"

Cecilia: "He knows how inconvenient it is here in winter, and having that great, large, lovely house in town, it's perfectly sweet and natural of him to—to, well, to ask—"

Tom: "Yes—you, to preside night after night at his deadly dinners, me to listen eternally to his delphic advice on what to do and how to live—in short, to allow him to own us. Of course, he's willing to pay. He always is."

Cecilia tells Tom that he is hard and unfeeling, but he replies:

"Hard? I'm not hard enough—that's the trouble with me. I never have been. I was brought up to dodge any truth—if it was unpleasant. In myself or anyone else—always be the little gentleman, Tommy —charming and agreeable at all costs—give no pain, Tommy."

When Tom finds what his marriage to Cecilia really amounts to and that he is being drawn back to the life from which he had escaped, he leaves her and returns to the unconventional but very alive group of people with whom he, as a writer, has been completely happy, and to the woman he has always loved.

Barry draws a very fine contrast between the world of set standards where a stifling atmosphere prevails, and one where convention and code, while fully understood, are not warping influences. While one does not infer that Barry is advocating the relationship that Tom and Daisy had had for years, he certainly shows that even this way of living is more decent than the disgusting marriage of Tom and Cecilia. However, the point is that Tom and Daisy should have been married from the beginning because they do love each other in every sense, but each felt that conventional ties would in some way hamper his or her work. This is like Jesse Lynch Williams' *Why Marry?* which draws the same conclusion, that two people who are really in love need not fear that marriage will alter their affection for each other.

Biography, by S. N. Behrman, produced at the Guild Theatre, December 12th, 1932, centers around an extremely attractive woman who is a successful portrait painter but whose life has been completely unconventional. And here one must pause for a moment to point out that this is a case where an individual has triumphed over the binding conventionalities, for Marion Froude has never considered convention seriously but has led her life just as it pleased her to lead it, and what is more to the point, she is *accepted* wherever she goes. It is ironic, but the secret is that she has been *successful* in her work. One can imagine, knows in fact, that straightlaced dowagers would whisper behind her back but one is equally certain that Marion would revel in hearing them. Her chief characteristic is tolerance, for she genuinely likes her fellow-men as a whole and when she meets an individual whom any other person might dislike intensely, she manages to be amused. When the play opens we see Marion in her New York studio where she has just arrived from a sojourn in Europe. From out of her early life comes Leander Nolan, or "Bunny," as Marion exasperatingly calls him. Horror stricken for fear she will mention him in the biography and kill his chances to be a senator he appeals to his backer, Orrin Kinnicott, a successful publisher. Both "Bunny," whose ideal in life is to be a senator, and Kinnicott, successful business man, are delightfully satirized. The former still clings to his small town outlook on life and can't get away from it. Marion's question, "Do you want to be a senator or can't you help it?" floats over his head, while her magnanimous offer couched in good humored ridicule, "I'll paint you, Bunny. Toga. Ferrule. Tribune of the people" loses its shafts in space.

The sickeningly conceited movie idol gets equally devastating treatment. When Warwick Wilson says he's making some personal appearances, Marion exclaims:

> "Personal appearances. I love that phrase. Has such an air of magnanimity about it."

Wilson replies that it *is* boring, perfect martyrdom, and that he has cramps from autographing books.

The deeper part of the play lies in the discussion between Marion and Kurt, who have fallen in love but, because of the total difference in their temperaments, cannot ever agree. It is a plea for tolerance but shows plainly why intolerance exists.

Kurt's secret dream is to be "critic-at-large of things-as-they-are." He wants to find out everything about the intimate structure of things and reduce the whole system to absurdity. Unlike Marion, he sees nothing that is noble, generous or gentle. Marion realizes that they can never agree and says to Kurt:

> "It was ourselves—the difference between us—not the years alone but the immutable differences in temperament. Your hates frighten me, Dickie. These people—poor Bunny, that ridiculous fellow Kinnicott—to you these rather ineffectual, blundering people symbolize the forces that have hurt you and you hate them. But I don't hate them. I can't hate them. Without feeling it, I can understand your hate but I can't bring myself to foster it"—

When "Dickie" finds out that Marion has destroyed the biography he exclaims:

> "I see now why everything is this way—why the injustice and cruelty go on—year after year—century after century—without change—because—as they grow older—people become—*tolerant!* Things amuse them. I hate you and I hate your tolerance. I always did."
>
> Marion: "I know you do. You hate my essential quality—the thing that is me. That's what I was thinking just now and that's what made me sad."

Society has been hard on Kurt, has defeated him because it has managed to shrivel his soul. We know that he will never rise out of the bitterness in which he has wrapped himself. And yet, he is less an object of pity than Mr. Kinnicott, who exercises daily, eats plenty of roughage and calls forth one of the most delightful comments of the play when he proudly announces that he has never changed his ways and Marion remarks that that is very nice, that if the world never changed either, "how consistent that would make you."

In *End of Summer*, produced at the Guild Theatre, New York, February 17th, 1936, Behrman delves into the question of wealth, its uses and misuses. The scene of the play is laid in the Frothinghams' summer home in Northern Maine. The grandmother, Mrs. Wyler, in the opening scene is talking to Will Dexter, a young radical who loves Paula Frothingham. Here we get the background of the family around whom the play revolves.

> Mrs. Wyler: "As I look back over my life the principal excitement came from houses—buying and building houses. The shack in Oil City to the mansion on Fifth Avenue. We had houses everywhere—houses in London, houses in Paris, Newport and this—and yet, it seemed to me, we were always checking in and out of hotels."

It is the picture of a wealthy family, never satisfied, always on the go, looking for something new and getting bored when the novelty has worn off.

Behrman takes the opportunity to reveal what the radical organizations of today's younger generation are doing. Two young men in the play are trying to start a paper but lack the necessary money. They are unwilling, at first, to accept the Frothinghams' help and all through the play show their resentment that a family could be so wealthy.

There is also a delightful bit of satire on psychoanalysts, just as in *Biography* the motion picture idol was satirized. Dr. Rice, formerly a nose and throat specialist, explains why he now delves into people's psychological reactions.

> "I devoted myself—when the victims would let me to their noses and throats. It was a starveling occupation. But I gave up tonsillectomy for the soul. The poor have tonsils but only the rich have souls. My instinct was justified—as you see."

Dr. Rice is an individual who has seized upon one of society's fads and who has turned it into a very lucrative channel for himself.

In the end, neither the young radical element nor the psychoanalyst attain their goals but we are told that when the Revolution comes, those who have financially assisted the revolutionists to overthrow the present order will be remembered. It is a consoling thought for all philanthropic capitalists .

The endless conflict between society and the individual is a theme which is always interesting to both playwright and audience. To begin with, it is dramatic, for it is one upon which intensely stirring scenes can be based. They are stirring because they are bound to touch the lives of everyone at some time or another. No matter whether the playwright takes up the study of an inherent weakness in an individual's character, as Clyde Fitch did, or whether he presents an individual fighting for certain rights as Barry did in *Holiday,* his play will have a direct appeal to an audience. Since there is no living person who is not in conflict with society in some aspect or another, plays which are concerned with this eternal struggle have a widespread interest.

There is more irony in the plays which belong to this particular phase of social comedy than there is in the plays which belong to the other phases. This is largely because the conflict of an individual with the social forces around him is frequently futile, or because, as in the case of *Expressing Willie,* he is trying to express something which doesn't exist. An individual cannot expect to shift the weight of responsibility that is justly his and defy social conventions successfully. This is obvious in Anspacher's *Unchastened Woman.* On the other hand, *Holiday* reveals that a person is justified to live as he pleases when he is not infringing upon other people's rights. Whatever aspect of life the different plays may touch, the fact remains that individuals are born with certain powers of their own which they may turn into either constructive or destructive forces. Furthermore, each person has to share in the responsibilities that society imposes upon him and he may be sure that when he tries to shift his share onto someone else, the whole weight of society will crush him. When an individual uses whatever attributes he possesses in a constructive form and triumphs over the obstacles that naturally confront him, society will generally recognize the victory.

D. THE CONFLICT BETWEEN THE GENERATIONS

The early American social comedies reflect a dutiful attitude on the part of children toward their parents. Especially is this true of daughters who generally accepted in marriage the man their parents had selected. They might protest and frequently did, but after being made to see how ungrateful this behavior was, they consented to marry their parents' choice. In less important matters they obeyed their elders with little question. For instance, they read only "nice" books, and they conducted themselves with the utmost propriety. This is evident in the first native social comedy, *The Contrast.*

Maria Van Rough dislikes intensely the affected fop, Dimple, but her father wishes her to marry him as he thinks Dimple is very wealthy. Maria has protested on the grounds that her mother married the man of her choice.

> Van Rough: "The man of her choice! And pray, Mary, an't you going to marry the man of your choice—what trumpery notion is this?—It is these vile books" (throwing them away). "I'd have you know, Mary, if you won't make young Van Dumpling the man of *your* choice, you shall marry him as the man of *my* choice."
>
> Maria: "You terrify me, Sir. Indeed, Sir, I am all submission. My will is yours."

Of course, Van Dumpling or Dimple, as he is called, turns out to be a wretch and Maria marries the man of her choice, but the conversation just quoted illustrates very clearly the attitude expected on the part of daughters.

James Nelson Barker's *Tears and Smiles,* produced in Philadelphia in 1807, again exemplifies the obedient daughter in the character of Louisa Campdon. Although inwardly rebelling against marrying a man whom she knows to be worthless, she consents to the marriage to please her father. However, an opportunity arises when she can, with the help of friends, reveal her fiancé in his true colors and she, like Maria, marries the man she loves.

We always feel reasonably sure that these young girls will not have to go to the altar with an object of distaste. In 1858, D. W. Wainwright's play, *Wheat and Chaff*, again discloses a dutiful daughter who bows to her mother's wishes in promising to marry a miserable fraud. Once more the villain is revealed in the nick of time. In *Young New York*, by E. G. P. Wilkins, produced in 1856, we discover that a daughter has defied her parents in the matter of choosing a husband and as a result is forced to leave home and make her own living. However, in these plays, as well as in most of the plays of Daly, such as *Lemons* (1877), when a son outwits his mother's plans for him; and in *The Railroad of Love* (1887), when a girl outwits her father with the aid of a friend, there is no real problem, but *The Last Word,* adapted by Daly from *Das Letzte Wort* of Franz von Schönthan and produced in 1890, contains a more serious view of this particular matter. The play has for its background Washington society and the social atmosphere of the Capital is very well established while the characterization is extremely well done. There are several very dramatic scenes with no descent into cither farce or melodrama. The interrelation between politics and social life is revealed clearly when the President politely asks the Secretary to go away for a long rest because the latter's daughter, Faith Rutherwell, has made an unfortunate choice of a husband. In a very dramatic scene she fools her father, who is about to announce her engagement to the man he wishes her to marry, and before the assembled guests, she goes to the man she loves, naming him as her future husband. There is a cloud over his diplomatic career at the moment which makes his position questionable.

The most interesting character in the play is a Russian baroness, Vera Boraneff, sister of Boris Bagoleff, the man Faith Rutherell loves and has chosen to marry. When Harry Rutherell, Faith's brother, comes to the Baroness's home to bring Faith back to her father and to try to persuade her to change her mind, Vera turns to him and says that she will talk to the Secretary.

Vera: "I shall venture to speak to him as I venture to
    say he has never been spoken to before—"
Harry: "But, Baroness, you don't know my father when
    he is angered."
Vera: "For that matter, he doesn't know me when I'm
    angered.   So we'll both have our little surprise."

Vera is full of dash and spirit and is the character upon whom
all the rest depend.   Through her, all difficulties are straightened
out in the end, of course, but the play is an excellent forerunner
of the independent attitude that women were beginning to take,
and of the coming revolution on the part of sons and daughters.

When, however, we turn to the post-war period of comedy and
take up the plays of Rachel Crothers and Philip Barry that center
around the theme of the conflict between the generations, we see
at once the difference in the treatment of this subject, for it has
now become a major problem.

An upheaval that shook society to its very foundations was what
has come to be called "the revolt of the younger generation."
After the World War had definitely proved that the term "civilization" is hardly more than a word, and a word with very little
meaning, the younger generation took matters into its own hands
and decided to investigate just what all the standards meant that
parents continually discussed.   If millions of people could go out
to slaughter each other, could destroy nearly every illusion one
held dear, then something was most assuredly wrong with the
laws by which society swore.   The revolt of the younger generation was a direct aftermath of the war not only because they were
disillusioned with life but because those who returned were keyed
up to a pitch which was not easy to discard for the regular routine
life at home.   This restlessness infected the people who had
remained at home, for they were naturally living under a strain
and in a state of excitement that war stirs up.   Furthermore, the
moral standards of those participating directly in the conflict
received a shock and in many instances were forgotten altogether.
So a combination of forces acted to overthrow one of the institutions precious to society, the obedience—or at least, reasonable
obedience—of younger people to their elders.   They began to

question every law by which their lives had been guided with the result that a perfect blaze of unconventionality swept over the country.

To begin with, "they believed in a greater degree of sex freedom than had been permitted by the strict American code; and as for discussion of sex, not only did they believe it should be free, but some of them appeared to believe it should be continuous."[3] Any sort of laws which in any way were restrictive they mocked. Prohibition, perhaps, stands as the most notable example in this instance. To defy it was an unalloyed delight. Before an alcohol shortage gripped the land boys and girls who were brought up in a "nice" manner thought little about drinking. At least, when the boys drank they did it at stag parties and looked down upon a girl who would toss off a strong drink as she would a glass of water. And it is equally true that a boy who appeared at a private ball or a country club dance intoxicated, or even with a strong odor of liquor on his breath, was flirting with social ostracism. It simply wasn't done and that was that. Naturally, when parents awoke to the incredible fact that their sons and daughters were haunting dimly lighted, smoke-filled speakeasies the shock was almost too much to bear. It was ghastly, particularly in the case of young ladies. But, argued this sex, they had to be good sports or they would be left sitting at home —and besides, they liked it! Nothing could be done, and on top of it all the feminine mode of dress passed beyond the bounds of the wildest imagination in the matter of abbreviation. The mid-Victorian lady wrapped in hypocrisy would not have fainted, as was her wont over any slight impropriety, but have *died,* had she beheld the modern young thing of the nineteen-twenties. Not that the Victorians didn't go to extremes which were ridiculous in their zeal for modesty when we remember that in America statues were draped to conceal Nature's art. "During those years the world was almost complex in its simplicity. The effort it made to deny reality was worthy of a better cause."[4] But one cannot deny that when the world suddenly decided to accept

---

[3] Allen, *Only Yesterday,* p. 234.
[4] Crouse, *Mr. Currier and Mr. Ives,* p. 73.

reality it did so with such violence that nothing short of a holocaust resulted.   The most unfortunate part of the revolt of the younger generation was the skepticism shown in the matter of religion. This does not apply, needless to say, to the younger people as a whole, but there was enough of it to cause general alarm.   However, this particular phase of the revolt seems to have afforded little satisfaction to those who so ardently adopted it for the time being.   This overturning of one of the fundamental laws which society complacently accepted for generations is reflected clearly in the later American social comedy.

Rachel Crothers is one of the most significant writers of American drama, both because of her sure theatrical sense and her accurate and understanding portrayal of human nature.   Until comparatively recently her work lay mainly in the field of domestic drama, but in 1920 with her production of *Nice People* she turned to social comedy.   This is a searching study and a sympathetic treatment of the "young rebels" who, after cutting loose, found themselves unable to make any sort of adjustment to their newly found freedom.   Unable to apply themselves to anything they spent their lives in a mad search for diversion.

Nice People shows what happened to the children in extremely wealthy families where money was handed to them without the remotest idea of how it was spent.   We see this careless parental attitude in the father of "Teddy," who hasn't the slightest idea of what his daughter is doing with her time or the money he lavishes upon her.   When he does realize what is going on it is practically too late, for she, like her friends, is now accustomed to managing her own life without having to account for it.   A good percentage of young people had reached the stage where if parents refused to allow them to do a thing they simply walked out of the house and did it regardless of objections.   Nearly all parents were termed "old fashioned" or were told that they had made a mess of the world and that it was time to try new standards.   The exaggerated importance that money suddenly commanded and how it lay at the base of any and every sort of decision is reflected in *Nice People* when one of the boys admits with appalling brazenness that he wouldn't consider marrying Teddy were it not for her money.

Education was ridiculed as much as money was lauded. To be really educated was almost a disgrace, for as Hallie, one of the girls puts it, it is "middle-class" to make one's education evident. She was educated in Paris where she was taught just enough to "appreciate everything in the world—but not to go far enough to be—you know," which fulfilled her mother's ambition for her.

"Of course," one of the boys rejoins, "appreciation is our vocation—appreciation of other people's work."

In a later discussion the question of conduct arises. Some of Teddy's friends think it better to conceal what they do, but Teddy, who is bluntly frank, says "you'll be talked about if you try to hide things. Do everything right before everybody's eyes—and dare them to talk." Her subsequent escapade, however, cures her of these extreme ideas.

Miss Crothers brings out the superficiality that smothers the essential fineness in people and makes them think that nothing is of any importance except *saying* that nothing matters. However, the close of the play reveals the inherent decency in people, with Teddy and her friends restored to a reasonable state because "the vital things of character don't belong to anybody's day—they're eternal and fundamental."

Again, in *Mary the Third,* produced at the 39th Street Theatre, New York, February 5th, 1923, there is the picture of a young girl who wants to try life for herself rather than follow the conventional standards that have been raised by the generations before her. However, this is only one theme of the play, for not only does Miss Crothers display conclusively that human nature is just the same now as it was in grandmother's day, but she scrutinizes mercilessly the state which many marriages reach when people just take each other for granted and drag out their existence together as a sort of wearisome duty.

First of all, we witness grandmother back in 1870 resorting to every known physical lure to capture the man she wants. Later, we see her daughter, who is a rather vacillating person, simply taking the man who is the more persistent of her two ardent admirers, and when Mary the third decides upon companionate marriage to see whether or not she really loves the boy who wants to make her his wife, she is simply reflecting the age in which she lives. Actually, her conduct hardly seems any worse, if as bad, as grandmother's, for she is less of a hypocrite. Convention, however, and a sense of duty toward her parents, triumphs, and she comes home. She overhears, however, a quarrel between her mother and father which destroys completely the respect she has had for something she now finds doesn't exist. Both she and her brother Robert are so aghast and horrified that they feel it would be far more respectable for their parents to separate. That they remain together is owing largely to force of habit, and the play ends in overwhelming irony when Mary the Third accepts her lover's proposal with the exact words her mother used;—"and we must make it the most wonderful love that was ever in the world."

A delightful touch in this play is grandmother's criticism of the thin and rather scanty clothes that Mary the third wears, whereupon the latter announces that no one of her generation would consider wearing a dress cut as low in front as those of grandmother's day, and that a backless one is far more respectable. This is not only indicative of Miss Crothers' understanding of human nature but shows that never so long as the world holds together will one generation approve of another. This play and *Nice People* are probably the best illustrations we possess in American dramatic literature of the direct conflict between the generations which keeps so many families in a constant state of turmoil.

In turning to the work of Philip Barry we find that he has taken up this same subject in several of his plays but considers it from a slightly different angle.

You and I (1923), which won for Barry the prize offered by Richard Herndon for the best play produced in the courses of Professor Baker at Harvard University, provides us with an unusually fine picture of a family whose members are devoted to each other but who recognize each other's rights. A certain flippant, but not disrespectful, attitude that they assume toward each other frequently hides what might easily descend into maudlin sentimentality. Barry's characters are always so perfectly sure

of social values that they can, at any time, launch into a certain
slang that never for one moment shakes one's faith in them but
on the contrary adds to their charm. Fundamentally they possess
a quiet assurance born of generations of good breeding. In *You
and I* the right of the younger people to make their own decisions
is respected by their parents and this in itself tells a social history,
a whole revolution in family customs, when we compare such a
condition with that which *The Contrast* and *Tears and Smiles*
reflected.

However, the difference in the outlook of the two generations
in *You and I* is not revealed by the fact that the parents allow
their son to make his own decisions, but in the contrast between
the woman of today and the woman of the last generation. Maitland White had always wanted to be an artist but when he married
Nancy he had to give up this idea and go into business. His son,
Ricky, wants to be an architect but requires two years of study
abroad. However, Ricky is in love with "Ronny" Duane and
decides to give up his two years abroad so that he can marry her
now. Like his father, he will go into business. "Ronny" tries
to prevent him from making this sacrifice for she knows that
Maitland White has never been happy in business and realizes
that Ricky will be equally dissatisfied as the years pass. It is
here that we see the difference in the generations. Nancy had
calmly let Maitland give up the idea of being an artist because for
her, marriage was the only career. Ronny Duane, on the other
hand, can turn to any one of the many new channels that have
opened for women. She is not dependent upon marriage as her
career but can enter the business world if she chooses. This contrast between the two generations is very clear and serves to
show the changing feminine standards.

Barry's next play, *The Youngest,* produced at the Gaiety Theatre, New York, December 22nd, 1924, holds up to ridicule the
Winslow family, leaders of a small town in New York State.
The youngest son, refusing to be smothered any longer by the
intolerable weight of family oppression, rebels. Probably nothing
sums up the play better than a remark made by Oliver Winslow,
the oldest of the brothers, when he says:

"I think we all realize that a family's standing in
its community is not a thing to be taken lightly."

This no one can deny, but when it becomes what might almost
be called an obsession there is no sight more ridiculous. The
smug and overwhelming complacency of the Winslows is both
ludicrous and pitiful. Each year, on the Fourth of July, the
inhabitants of the small town in which the Winslows live come
en masse to hear Oliver make a dull and heavy speech in which
he impresses upon them the true American spirit. He exhorts
the workers in the Winslow pin factory to greater zest but on this
particular Fourth of July, Richard, the youngest son, tears up the
speech and Oliver is helpless for he has no originality. Richard
then takes the reins and gives the crowd a treat, for which it is
totally unprepared, but which wins uproarious applause. It is a
scene one cannot forget. While the play is not by any means
one of Barry's best, nevertheless it might benefit many families
either to see or to read it.

White Wings was not understood by the public when it was
produced in 1926 at the Booth Theatre, New York. With the
horse as the symbol of stubborn family pride which is unwilling
to acknowledge any advance or improvement in life, and the automobile as the symbol of progress, Barry has given us a particularly
keen study in social contrasts. The Inch family have been White
Wings or street cleaning contractors for many generations. Between them and the Todds a feud develops, for a member of the
Todd family has invented the automobile, which will drive the
horse, which the Inches worship, from the streets. The grim
desperation with which the Inches fight a losing battle, despite its
absurdity, arouses our admiration while Barry's handling of the
situation keeps our sympathy entirely with them. Tragic, and
filled with pathos is the last scene when old Mr. Inch has to get
into a garbage truck, his colors lowered at last. The tone of the
play from beginning to end is high comedy and one might safely
say that never has family pride been more delightfully exposed.

The conflict between the generations is, like the conflict between
society and the individual, one which has been going on since time

immemorial. Whether, as in the earliest American social comedies, the younger generation conceals much of the rebellious feeling that arises, or whether this feeling bursts forth as in the plays of Miss Crothers, the conflict is there just the same. What is of particular interest to us, however, is the freedom that the younger people of today exercise in contrast to those of a hundred and more years ago. This is again largely owing to the difference in woman's position. Throughout the social comedies which center around the conflict between the generations there is noticeable a steady growth of freedom on the part of the younger people. In the beginning we see daughters bowing to their parents' will. Later, they do everything they can to outwit them and there are a few cases of actual defiance. Finally, after the war, we see them cast aside all semblance of obedience and ignore their parents completely. They are searching for new values and standards upon which to base their lives for they feel that the old ones have not been satisfactory. Invariably, the pendulum always swings too far in one direction during a period of unrest like that of the nineteen twenties but when people have had enough excitement they retreat to a more moderate course. In the plays of Miss Crothers we find the younger people discovering that there is very little in their wild search for diversion. Barry does not take up this theme but shows the opposing viewpoints of the generations. *White Wings* is symbolic of a static condition as opposed to progress. The choice of the horse and the automobile to represent these two aspects of life is a particularly happy one. Just what angle the future American playwrights will present when they deal with the different generations is a question we cannot answer, but we may be sure that there will be a conflict. Miss Crothers, at least, in *Mary the Third* settles definitely the theory that several generations cannot live in peace under the same roof.

E. SOCIETY AND THE INSTITUTIONS OF MARRIAGE AND DIVORCE

Probably no factor has contributed more to a fundamental change in the standards of society than the difference in the status of woman today from what it was before the Civil War. While it is true that woman used to occupy an imaginary pedestal and during the Victorian Age was regarded as a fragile creature, this particular advantage seems to be about the only one to which she could lay claim. During the courtship leading up to the great moment when the ardent lover consulted first the father, then asked the girl herself, and in turn had to go back to the father, she was always regarded as a frail flower but when once married she was not always treated with so much consideration. Today a woman can walk out of the house and get a divorce if her husband is a drunkard or a libertine but until the time when divorce was no longer considered a disgrace, she remained tied to whatever lot she had drawn. Before the Civil War no respectable woman considered getting a divorce and if she did, as happened in a few cases, she lost the custody of her children. It is really to the industrial revolution that woman owes her emancipation, for as industry increased on an ever widening scale, there were more and more positions which women seemed better fitted to fill than men. When women with assured social standing began gradually to break down the taboo against members of their sex entering the business world, their real freedom began, and with this freedom and financial independence came an upheaval in one of the most fundamental laws of society and a decided blow to many conventions held dear for generations. Naturally, an important social change of this kind became a subject for both novelists and dramatists, and writers are still wielding their pens with great zeal, either defending or denouncing divorce, upholding woman's right to do as she pleases or crying out against her for aggressiveness. In the field of drama Augustin Daly was one of the first to take up the question of divorce and in 1871 produced a play bearing that title.

Divorce is an argument for the preservation of the family institution, an institution upon which society is fundamentally based. Fanny Ten Eyck, the central figure of the play, has married a man whom she loves but his unreasonable jealousy, which he cannot control, has caused a serious breach between them. They finally separate, Fanny taking their child with her to her mother's. The play becomes melodrama when the father, deranged mentally, kidnaps the child and Fanny goes to the hiding place to bring the child home. When he is cured of his mental trouble Fanny goes to see her husband, taking the child along and, of course, the little boy is the cause of their reunion.

The growing independence of women is shown by Fanny's attitude when her husband forbids her to see an elderly admirer. Not in the least in love with this man, Fanny sees no reason to stop him from coming to her house and is openly defiant. Mrs. Kemp, Fanny's aunt, tries to make peace between husband and wife and in the following conversation we see the difference in the position of women in Mrs. Kemp's day and that of Fanny. The former is giving Fanny advice:

> Fanny: "Advise me to do what? I have already done everything he wishes."
> Mrs. Kemp: "But things are worse than ever!"
> Fanny: "That is his fault."
> Mrs. Kemp: "You have not implicitly obeyed his wishes."
> Fanny: "Don't use that word to me, I can't bear it."
> Mrs. Kemp: "Why, my dear, it's the duty of a true wife."
> Fanny: "Right or wrong?"
> Mrs. Kemp: "Right or wrong."
> Fanny: "This is your doctrine?"
> Mrs. Kemp: "I have lived by it forty years."
> Fanny: "Then listen to mine. Just so far as it is right I will obey his wishes. If I am in doubt, I will give him the benefit of that doubt and still comply, but if he outrages my feelings, insults my friends and suspects my honor, I will resent it with all my power to the day of my death."

In spite of the determined stand which Fanny, with some reason, has taken she still gives in to her husband far more than the present-day wife is pictured as doing. Very seldom do we see the man being given the benefit of the doubt by a sweetly smiling, meek wife, whose creed is obedience to her husband.

The seriousness of the main plot is off-set by two minor ones, one of which concerns Lu Ten Eyck, Fanny's sister, who has married a man years older than she and who is bored with him. She tries every conceivable excuse to get a divorce and in this particular case, the whole subject is satirized to the point of being made ridiculous. Unfortunately, women like Lu Ten Eyck exist and try to conjure up in their imaginations terrible abuses on the part of devoted husbands so that, farcical though this minor plot is, it has a few grains of truth in it. As a whole, the play is the first to probe deeply into the question of divorce and marriage and to show the relationship between these two institutions and the social laws which are an integral part of them. The futility of divorce in the majority of cases becomes apparent for in most instances an individual's position is weakened rather than strengthened.

During the first decade of the twentieth century one of the most brilliant plays in the history of American social comedy centered around the problems that arise in society when marriages crash and divorce follows. The complete assurance that the characters in this play possess entitles them to scoff at convention when they choose, although not one of them would permit of an actual infringement. It is here that much of the humor in social comedy arises, for we thoroughly enjoy a certain daring in people who can afford to indulge in it.

Langdon Mitchell's *New York Idea* was presented at the Lyric Theatre, New York, on November 19th, 1906. It is an example of social comedy at its best, for the playwright, while dealing with the institution of divorce, does so with an air of complete detachment. The situations in which individuals find themselves because of our divorce laws; and the effect of the laws upon them he skillfully portrays through a plot which, were it not for the almost incomparable brilliance of the dialogue, would at times hardly hold together. One of the chief sources of amusement is the fact that Mitchell seizes upon a painfully conventional family and proceeds to heap upon its most conservative members one shock after another. The lack of any really serious purpose in the lives of people with no responsibilities is reflected in John and Cynthia Karslake, who have been divorced after a very short marriage but who still love each other intensely. The futility of the modern idea of hurrying to court to obtain a divorce if you disagree upon a few things is clearly revealed. The uncomfortable and embarrassing situations that arise when people who move in the same circle socially are necessarily thrown together after they have separated, provide much of the humor in the play.

Cynthia Karslake is engaged to marry Philip Phillimore and is ensconced behind the Phillimore tea table when Vida, Philip's former wife, enters. She has, of course, come to see what her successor is like but pretends at first that she has come on some business. Philip is much upset over the performance and feels that Cynthia should leave the room.

> Cynthia: (Determined not to leave the field first, remains seated) "Certainly, Philip!"
> Philip: "I expect another visitor who—"
> Vida: (With flattering insistence, to Cynthia) "Oh, my dear—don't go! The truth is—I came to see you! I feel most cordially towards you—and really, you know, people in our position should meet on cordial terms."
> Cynthia: (Taking it with apparent calm, but pointing her remarks) "Naturally. If people in our position couldn't meet, New York society would soon come to an end."
> (Enter Thomas).
> Vida: (Calm, but getting her knife in too) "Precisely. Society's no bigger than a band-box. Why, it's only a moment ago I saw Mr. Karslake walking—"
> Cynthia: "Ah!"
> Thomas: (Announcing clearly. Everyone changes place, in consternation, amusement or surprise. Cynthia moves to leave the stage, but stops for fear of attracting Karslake's attention.) "Mr. John Karslake!"

After continued embarrassment and strained conversation, Sir Wilfrid Cates-Darby, an Englishman, is introduced. He is completely confused when he finds that Mrs. Karslake is no longer the wife of Mr. Karslake and that Mrs. Phillimore is no longer the wife of Mr. Phillimore, but they finally reveal the situation to him. The light way in which Americans look upon divorce has made an impression however, and he exclaims to Cynthia:

"Damme, my dear lady, a marriage in your country is no more than a-eh-h-what do you call 'em? A 'thank you, ma'am.' That's what an American marriage is—a 'thank you, ma'am.' Bump—bump —you're over it and on to the next."

It is this lightness of nature that Mitchell seizes upon to satirize, for he says that what he wanted to satirize was a "certain extreme frivolity in the American life—frivolity in the deep sense—not just a girl's frivolity, but that profound, sterile, amazing frivolity which one observes and meets in our churches, in our political life, in literature, in music. . . . Our frivolity is, I feel, on the edge of the tragic. Indeed, I think it is entirely tragic, and there are lines, comedy lines, in *The New York Idea* that indicate this aspect of the thing." Thus, beneath the brilliant surface of the play there is a very definite and serious motive for the author's having written it. This contrast between individuals who respect social values almost to the point of standing in awe of them, and those who, while fully aware of them, enjoy mocking them occasionally, is one of the fundamental characteristics of society everywhere.

When one remembers the attitude toward divorce that existed thirty years before this play he can readily see the tremendous change that had swept over society. Not only did divorce give one a doubtful reputation but it plunged every branch of a family into a state of uneasiness. To say that there had been a divorce in a family was to uncover a very unpleasant matter indeed. It was a skeleton that relatives wished kept securely locked in its closet. Man and wife were expected to live together for "better or for worse." About the only respectable way for a woman to leave her husband was to die. Probably no better example of this attitude can be found than in Edith Wharton's *The Age of Innocence* where, owing to the weight of the opinion of the tribe, a woman decides against divorce. Today, in a case of the kind described in the novel, divorce would seem both more respectable and just. However, what Mitchell was pointing out in *New York Idea* was that the pendulum had swung too far toward a careless leniency.

A charming play in which we see the changing feminine attitude from Victorianism to modern standards is *A Woman's Way*, by Thompson Buchanan, first presented by Grace George on January 7th, 1909, in Milwaukee, Wisconsin, and then in New York the same winter on February the 22nd at the Hackett, now the Harris Theatre.   Marion and Howard Stanton have begun to drift in different directions, she becoming more and more active socially while her husband has become involved in racing and consequently with an entirely different group of people.   An affair he has been having with a Mrs. Blackmore comes to light because of an automobile accident.   Marion determines to fight to win him back, thus shocking her father, who wants her to come home; while at the same time she proceeds to startle her husband, Howard, by making unconventional statements concerning the accident.   She also arouses his jealousy through the aid of Oliver Whitney, a charming bachelor.   They pretend to be engrossed in each other whenever Howard is in sight.   Bright and sophisticated though she is, she is not a woman of Mrs. Blackmore's experience, which seems boundless.   However, her remarkable handling of a difficult situation and her never-failing presence of mind triumph in the end.   The stand she takes seems to be a good compromise between the extreme modern way, in which case she would very likely have turned to other men and the old-fashioned principles, according to which she would have rushed home in tears to her parents.   The ethical code of the men is questionable, to say the least, but as Buchanan has drawn them, they are a group of very human, amusing and not at all unpleasant beings.   Their embarassment upon meeting Mrs. Blackmore and their deadly fear of having their wives discover that they have *all* known her before, is one of the high points of the play.

In this play we see a woman meet an extremely unpleasant and embarrassing situation and triumph over it with her colors still flying.   She *knows* that her husband loves her and she *knows* that she loves him.   The divorce her family wishes her to get never materializes.   Never for one moment does she lose a single quality belonging to a gentlewoman but remains perfectly poised throughout the entire trial she endures.   This is what actually defeats her rival so completely. The contrast between these two women is unusually fine.

The Rainbow, by A. E. Thomas, was produced at the Liberty Theatre, New York, on March 4th, 1912. It centers around two divorced people who are eventually reunited by their daughter, Cynthia. An extremely vivid and memorable portrait of an elderly man with plenty of money who has nothing to do but exist, impresses itself upon us when Neil Sumner, remarking upon the old gentleman's sartorial perfection, adds:

> "Year by year getting a little plumper, a little balder, a little more sallow, a little more wheezy, a little more selfish year after year. Some morning his valet will call him for his bath at nine o'clock as usual—and—well—he won't wake up. Hm!—I wonder if there isn't anything more in life than that."

Equally unpleasant is the glimpse we get of the racing crowd, composed of disillusioned, burned out people who can no longer find any real pleasure in life. Thomas has again picked out a particular element of society and revealed it for what it is worth. Again the tragedy of divorce in certain cases is brought out in an understanding and sympathetic manner.

Needless to say there are many ways of looking upon marriage. It may be a business, a lark, a convenience, or something very sacred and beautiful. However, most people have very likely never thought of it as a game, or at least a diverting game, but Anne Crawford Flexner in her comedy,' *The Marriage Game* (1913) shows us just how it may be played. The scene is a yacht, the characters a group of wretched married people, until a mysterious Mrs. Oliver, who at first arouses the jealousy of all the wives, shows them how to keep their husbands. This she does quite simply, by referring to Disraeli's remark to his wife: "You are more like a mistress than a wife!" which, says Mrs. Oliver, is the highest compliment a man can pay his wife. Although the compliment at first has a startling sound, upon reflection it is not hard to find the real meaning that lies beneath it and we must agree with Mrs. Oliver that it *is* a compliment indeed. The play satirizes women who are bridge fiends, women who try to force bad health upon their husbands to prevent them from doing what they enjoy, and women with jealous natures who instantly misunderstand anything and everything. In other words, they do whatever they can to make themselves as unattractive as possible to their husbands, instead of playing the role of a mistress, who never fails, if she can help it, to do what pleases a man most and who always tries to look her best for him. The manner in which the various types of wives are assembled and have a chance to show themselves in their true light is very well done. The play is clever, if not important, and has an aspect that husbands at least can appreciate—especially present day ones.

The Better Understanding (1917), which A. E. Thomas wrote in collaboration with Clayton Hamilton is a penetrating study of a woman who feels neglected because of her husband's absorption in business, and who is jealous of his preoccupation. She is on the verge of running away with a man whom she has known since childhood and who has always loved her. However, in a very powerful and moving scene, her husband wins her back. There is throughout the play a particularly fine sense of honor, of the fundamental social standards against which the characters refuse to rebel. Also, the difference in the love that the woman feels for her husband and the love that she feels for the other man is very well shown. What she wants more than anything on earth is her husband's love and affection and she is one of those individuals whose nature requires this. Consequently, when little comes to her she is almost driven to another man, but a "better understanding" saves her and her husband's marriage from ruin. This lack of understanding on the part of so many people as to each other's feelings is really the basis of the play. The man may be too preoccupied with business or the woman with either her children or some outside interest to realize the barrier that is gradually growing between them. Then, as in the play just discussed—one of them—here it is the wife—will be too proud to reveal the deeper feelings that lie hidden, and by the time this finally happens it is frequently too late.

A play which was far in advance of its time and which caused a great deal of comment when it was produced is Jesse Lynch Williams' comedy, *Why Marry?*, first entitled *And So They Were Married*. It made its appearance at the Astor Theatre, New York, on December 25th, 1917. Here we have a frank and penetrating scrutiny of marriage as an institution. Marriage as a career, marriage which is little more than legalized prostitution and companionate marriage are all considered in turn. According to Williams, the audience at first received the play in cold disapproval, owing to the daring nature of its subject, but when the people saw the humor which runs throughout the play they changed their attitude and it became a decided success.

The successful but extremely obnoxious business man who believes that nothing can be gotten without money, including affection and love, because he can't think of, and probably doesn't know of any other way, is very well presented. His wife despises him but is too weak to kick over the traces and divorce him. In the first scene his younger sister succeeds in enticing the son of wealthy neighbors to propose to her since, as she says, she "has been brought up to be married and nothing else." Actually, she is in love with another man but he is poor, which means that she will have to wait for a long time. Helen, the older sister, is assistant to a scientist, Ernest Hamilton, whom she loves and who loves her. With the example of her family before them they have decided that they will dispense with the marriage ceremony, as they feel that to be married will ruin their careers, and besides, they do not need any vows to bring them together but will live more happily together without them. One is almost inclined to share their viewpoint, but as Helen's uncle, Judge Grey, points out; "Bad as marriage is, until we reform it, it is the best we have to offer you." The play is brilliant throughout, the dialogue almost too swift at times for one to catch its full meaning. Furthermore, the characters never for a moment lose their sense of values but they question the codes by which they have been living.

Why Not?, the play which followed *Why Marry?*, Williams describes as a "comedy of conventions." It treats "divorce with philosophic levity (as in *Why Marry?*), superimposed upon a soundly reasoned protest against existing divorce laws and the accepted conventions surrounding the correction of marital mistakes." *Why Not?* was produced at the 48th Street Theatre, December 25th, 1922.

In the play are two couples who decide to exchange mates with each other; Leonard and Mary Chadwick and Bill and Evadne Thompson. Churchill Smith, a lawyer, is trying to tell them how scandalous it would be were they to divorce each other, change mates and remarry.

> Smith: "But how about your marriage vows? 'Whom God hath joined together'."
> Evadne: "But God didn't join Bill and me together. Man did."
> Smith: "What?"
> Evadne: "Man's semi-civilized ideas about money and matrimony. The world, not God, persuaded Bill and me that we'd make what the world calls a 'suitable match'."
> Leonard, beside Evadne: "God did his best to join *us* together."
> Bill, beside Mary: "And Mary and me."
> Leonard: "Why else should God grant us humans the divine gift of love? This is what he intended in the first place. We disobeyed God."
> Smith, regaining his good humor: "Then pay the penalty."
> Leonard: "We have paid the penalty—fifteen years' imprisonment."
> Smith: "But marriage is a life sentence!"
> Bill: "To be commuted by divorce—released for good behavior."
> Mary: "And that's all there is to it."

By way of showing them grounds for divorce Smith tells them that a couple whom they know is getting a "perfectly proper divorce" because of unfaithfulness. Later they find that the woman has forgiven her husband for the sake of the children. As Evadne puts it, their children must appreciate being "reared in an atmosphere of sin and mutual contempt."

In the end, Bill, Evadne, Leonard and Mary, having gotten divorces and remarried all decide to live in the same house together because of *their* children. Smith again speaks to them regarding this arrangement.

> Smith: "But nice people won't understand."
> Leonard: "Nice people never do—let 'em rave."

The whole play shows up the many absurdities connected with our divorce laws, especially when adultery is pointed out as being the best grounds for separation. Although, as we have seen, Williams' plays were considered very advanced for their time, he can never be accused of letting his characters overstep the limits of good breeding either in their actions or their speech. The dialogue always represents that of well-bred, conventional people to whom anything that is not mentioned simply does not exist. In this instance Williams and Mitchell are much alike but the difference between their plays lies in the fact that Williams very obviously chooses a definite institution or convention and questions it, while Mitchell argues neither for nor against any institutions or conventions. Primarily, he is interested in his characters and the situations that result from their actions.

Lee Wilson Dodd's *The Changelings,* produced September 17th, 1923, is in one aspect similar to Williams' *Why Not?* We again see two married couples who discover that if they exchanged mates they would be better suited to each other. One husband and the wife of the other man are "old-fashioned" while the other two are very "modern." They have never actually realized this fully until Wicky Faber, son of one couple, comes home to announce that his wife, Kay, daughter of the other couple, has left him. The different reactions on the part of the four parents discloses their real natures to each other and affords a highly amusing scene. The action becomes farcical at times but the underlying theme is sound and rather illuminating. Unlike Williams' *Why Not?* the two couples remain in their original marital state but one senses that never again will any of them feel quite the same toward one another.

The battle between the conventional outlook of society and the unconventional behavior on the part of the individual is very well drawn. For years each couple has lived along together and in neither case has either individual really understood the other. The two conventional members of the quartet are the more sympathetic characters, for the other two are defeated by their advanced ideas, which prove useless in a crisis. The children are reunited and in the last scene we witness the "changelings" playing the role of contented grandparents.

Gilbert Emery has contributed a brilliant comedy of manners to the American stage. *Episode,* produced in 1925, shows the helpless position in which a man finds himself when he discovers that his wife has been the mistress of his best friend and he can say nothing without ruining the happiness of his friend's wife. The original title of the play was "Saving Judy," for it is to spare Judy Ballinger from the knowledge that her husband, Herbert, and Eve Ryesdale have been lovers that Herbert, Eve and Arnold Ryesdale act as they do in the final scene of the play.

Eve Ryesdale is a very attractive woman and one who wants to get all the fun there is out of life but, as we gather from a telephone conversation in the first part of the play, she has found little fun with her husband, Arnold. This conversation is a priceless and vivid picture of a certain element in society. The telephone rings and Eve answers it.

> Eve: "Hello—hello—Judy Ballinger, you lamb! What? I can't hear a word for this hellish racket going on in the telephone,—What?—Why, of course I'm coming. My dear, I wouldn't miss it. I'm mad to see the Polo and the Prince and you and—my dear, hasn't he the sweetest manners you ever saw? You heard about the Peters' luncheon for him, didn't you?—Yes, I was there. My child, the Prince was in a *corner,* in a *tent,* entirely surrounded by all those gold-lined Peterses, and the servants marched by, carrying great *trenchers* of rich, luscious food; and if you tried to get as much as an olive, they shouted 'This is for the Prince!' People like us were taken home in ambulances starving.—What? Why I thought I'd have a puppy-biscuit here and

> then motor down afterwards and—Who? Arnold?
> Oh, no, of course not. You can't pry him out, not
> with ice-tongs. He never goes anywhere, Judy,
> except to *reunions of relatives.* I did ask him. I
> implored. I told him *you* wanted him *especially.*
> But, oh no! Business! Too busy! My dear, his
> idea of an outing is to go and sit, all alone, in a nice,
> cosy, safety-deposit vault in his bank with a large
> rich *bond* in either hand—I said *bond, not bun*—."

This establishes the whole background of the Ryesdale's life
both public and private. We see at once the difference in their
temperaments, Arnold devoted to business to the exclusion of
nearly everything else while Eve, in order to offset the otherwise
unendurable monotony of her life, goes everywhere. She has,
also, a certain spontaneity and gayety that Arnold can't understand. However, to the outside world their marriage is what
would very likely be termed a "great success"—Eve, charming
socially, Arnold, successful in business. It is Eve's almost incredible poise that keeps the tense situation into which she, Arnold
and Herbert Ballinger are plunged from becoming melodramatic.
Added to that, of course, is their heritage of good breeding which
instills in them an inherent dislike of a scene. It is this restraint,
this natural sense of what is required of them by their social code,
that raises the play to the high level it maintains. Arnold at first
refuses to go with Eve and Herbert to the latter's house where
Judy is waiting for them. Throughout the scene Eve has been
trying to save Judy from finding out about her and Herbert.

> Eve (to Arnold): "But, my dear man, what excuse
> have I to offer Judy, if you don't go? Obviously,
> you can't be ill. Obviously, I should say, it can't
> be business for if it *were* business, you'd have told
> her yourself over the telephone, *wouldn't* you? She
> expects us to start at once—so whatever happens,
> must happen at once—Well, what is it to be?
> Decide, Arnold!"
> - - - - - -
> Ryesdale: "Say what you like! Say what you please!
> Only get out of here, both of you, and leave me
> alone."

Eve: "Well, Arnold, in that case I shall say to Judy—nothing."

Ryesdale: "You mean—What do you mean? Nothing." (Ballinger, who has been sunk in his gloomy thoughts, now looks up in horror)

Eve: "I repeat—nothing. That is, beyond saying to Judy that you refused flatly to come, and that *you will tell her why.*"

Ryesdale: "Even you wouldn't dare that."

Eve, firmly: "Arnold, I give you my word that's what I'll say—that and only that—if I go."

Ballinger, with a groan: "That'll fix it all right."

Ryesdale to Eve: "I'd believe anything of you now."

Eve: "You can see what that will precipitate, can't you? In Judy's case."

- - - - - -

- - - - - -

Ryesdale: "Do you realize that you are stripping a situation which demands fineness of feeling, a—a—sense of decency, a sense of—of *shame,* that you're stripping it of every vestige of dignity?"

Eve: "Herbert doesn't look so very dignified. Neither do you. Your tie is on one side. And your face is very red. I don't expect I look much better, though I've certainly tried to keep calm and not let my nose get shiny. Is it shiny?"

Ryesdale, beside himself: "Ballinger, won't you ask her, for God's sake, to behave like—like—"

Eve, helping him out pleasantly: "A woman of sin, Arnold?"

Finally Eve tells Arnold how deadly her life has been because he really never stopped to think about her but has taken her for granted. "I became Mrs. Arnold Ryesdale and your sister Ella got me into after-war reconstruction work—and a fallen Women's Club. And when that petered out there wasn't anything left except what was left—only a good deal more so." Then she tells how Herbert Ballinger seemed a hero to her when he returned from game shooting in Africa and how Arnold did nothing for her except point out how "damnable" their life was getting to be. "I don't quite know how you could have helped me, Arnold, but I've got a kind of feeling you might have—some way—I expect the trouble was I was bored."

In the end, Eve and Herbert leave to join Judy while Arnold promises to follow them later. The force of habit in keeping up appearances that society has impressed upon them, and the desire to keep Judy in ignorance of what has happened causes all three of them to carry on for the time being. However, we know that Eve and Arnold are going to separate.

The play, like Edith Wharton's novel, *The House of Mirth*, is a glimpse behind the scenes of conventional society. We see how people go on regardless of what may have occurred, for the sake of appearances; how they are ruled by forces outside of themselves. Their lives are cast into one certain mold within the bounds of which they must live, and when they break through these bounds the laws of society will censure them.

Paris Bound, by Philip Barry, was produced on December 27th, 1927, at the Music Box Theatre in New York. Barry takes the same stand that Daly had taken in 1871 but, of course, the atmosphere and tone are different, owing to the more modern outlook of the characters. Fundamentally, however, the play is based on the same theory, the preservation of the institution of the family. At the opening of the play Jim and Mary Hutton, while waiting for the signal to rush from the house to start on their honeymoon, discuss their future together. Mary says that first of all they must "respect each other's privacy" and that they must both see other people a great deal so that they will never tire of each other. Jim considers this "nice and sensible and modern." Later, however, when Mary finds that Jim has not been true to her, her first impulse is to get a divorce, until she finds that she too can be interested in another man yet *love* only Jim and their children. When Mary makes the discovery about Jim she talks it over with James Hutton, Jim's father, who tries to persuade her not to wreck her home by getting a divorce but she is determined to do so. He tells her that she has based hers and Jim's life upon a physical basis alone if she is willing to smash everything because of Jim's relations with the other girl. Mary denies this vehemently and finally ends the argument by politely but firmly hinting that she wishes to be alone.

Barry brings out the tragedy that so often follows divorce in the characters of Jim Hutton's parents who meet for the first time in fifteen years at their son's wedding.   The strong emotion and deep feeling that the wedding is stirring up in them come to the surface although they try to conceal the fact in light conversation for a time.   At one point, however, both reach the breaking point but are interrupted by the appearance of other persons.   This scene reveals Barry's ability to disclose by a mere touch or word what many playwrights would express in a manner that would make us writhe in sheer embarrassment.   It is because Barry is perfectly sure of himself that his characters in this particular field of comedy behave like civilized beings instead of giving way to their feelings.   The clever manner in which he checks James and Helen in their growing anger adds credit to his artistry. James Hutton, after the years that have intervened, still tries to show Helen the mistake she made by leaving him, tries to show her how miserable both have been and what they have missed by not being able to watch their son grow up together.   From a very few words we grasp the whole background of their lives; Helen "successfully" married to an Englishman whom she probably likes and respects but doesn't love, and her divorced husband living out a rather embittered life, finding his only real happiness in his son Jim, and now in both Jim and Mary.   It is true that when Mary faces the same situation that confronted Helen and impulsively decides to leave Jim one has every sympathy for her because, not mentioning her hurt pride and the perfectly natural grief that she suffers, Jim has broken one of the standards by which society distinguishes between decency and indecency, between morality and immorality.   Without this law there would be no society but a reversal to primitive conditions which is hardly different from animal life.   But because we know that, despite his misdemeanor, Jim is in love with Mary, is devoted to his children and is essentially fine, we side with the playwright in his view that to destroy completely a family because of an act that in this case does not actually bring real harm to any of its members, is a far greater wrong than Jim's behavior.   However, we must also admit that it does seem to boil down to a choice between the lesser of

two evils. But Barry, like Daly, upholds the institution of the
family as the rock upon which society must stand or fall.

Here one must pause to consider the influence that a playwright's religious creed has upon his work. Both Barry and Daly
naturally uphold the laws of the Catholic Church. A strict moral
code exists in the Catholic home, while the family unit is always
held foremost. Consequently, these two playwrights lay emphasis
upon the importance of the institution of the family as the greatest
bulwark against the moral breakdown of society. The essential
importance of the family unit and devotion to the Church are two
of the fundamentals upon which Catholicism is based. An offense
against either of these institutions is considered not only a religious
breakdown, but a weakening of civilization itself. It is this breaking down of faith in and loyalty to the home above all other social
institutions that the plays of Daly and Barry fight against. A
man and woman must strive for the sake of preserving the family
to rise above the forces that would destroy their marriage. If
they do this they strengthen the fundamental structure of society.

The glittering and sparkling light comedy of *Paris Bound*
depends upon several minor characters, one of whom, Fanny Ship-
pan, sails in and out with a delightful flippancy that completely
disarms us. She stands in awe of nothing for she is "the ninth
richest woman under thirty in North America." Europe means
very little to her except a place to go for a change of scenery
occasionally. Upon being asked whether she was presented at
court in England, she replies: "James, I was there with ostrich
plumes in my hair. It was a riot. The queen swooned, and the
king was carried out screaming."

Fanny is very American and glad of it even though she stayed
abroad long enough to have a salon.

> "I had a salon. I honestly had a salon. I can't
> tell you what I've been through. Last night when
> I saw Fifth Avenue, I cried into my lap for fully
> twenty minutes. It's a nice little city you've got
> here, friends. It's going to grow. You're not really
> sailing for that place today?"

An attitude like this toward Europe is so completely different from that portrayed in the earlier plays of the nineteenth century that one can hardly believe the plays are written by dramatists of the same country. Of course, the earlier social comedies were, as we have seen, largely satires on the parvenu while Barry's comedies deal with people who find it unnecessary to imitate or stand in awe of anyone or anything. Furthermore, they are very human and real, possessing decided individuality. In *Paris Bound* there are a number of people around the same age but instead of being types each one is most definitely a human being with qualities that distinguish him or her from the others.

Rachel Crothers has written two plays, both of which take up the theme found in *Paris Bound*. In *Let Us Be Gay* (1929), Miss Crothers has given us a fine study not only of divorce but of a group of people who, largely through boredom, have lost practically all sense of values. The play centers around two people, Kitty and Bob Brown, who are divorced but who still love each other deeply. In the end they are reunited because during their separation they have learned the real meaning of their love and their marriage. Mrs. Boucicault, an elderly woman whose house is a mecca for week-end pleasure seekers, reveals the difference between her generation and the modern one when she describes her concern over her granddaughter who is having an affair with a married man.

> "I always knew my husband wasn't faithful to me, but I lived in hell with him for fifty years, because divorce wasn't respectable. My only daughter had three divorces—which I was tickled to death to see her get—and here's my grandchild in the middle this modern revolution and I'm helpless—can' a thing for her."

While Mrs. Boucicault obviously approves of at a loss over what seems the complete upsetti social convention. However, she invites week-end house party in order to have Ki her granddaughter. Of course, she do

Bob are divorced, nor will Kitty let Bob tell anyone. The use of a social occasion such as a house party makes plausible the meeting between Bob and Kitty, who might otherwise never have seen each other again. A social gathering of this kind is frequently the factor which determines whether a play be domestic or social comedy. The central problem in *Let Us Be Gay* is domestic, but its background of standards makes it social comedy.

On October 6th, 1932, *When Ladies Meet* opened at the Royale Theatre, New York. In this play Miss Crothers placed before the audience the moral standards that men expect women to preserve and the moral standards that women expect men to uphold. When the play was produced in Philadelphia, one of the reviewers for a certain paper apparently had sat through the play without ever grasping the point, for his interpretation stressed not the word "ladies" in the title, but the word "meet." The two women involved are gentlewomen and in their instant recognition of this quality in each other lies the importance of the play.

Mary Howard is writing a novel with the central situation revolving around the eternal triangle. A married man has fallen in love with another woman and wishes to divorce his wife. Mary feels that if the woman will go to the wife and explain just how matters stand, the wife will be broadminded and understanding enough to give up her husband. Actually, this is the situation in which Mary herself has become involved. When she tells the plot of her book to Jimmie Lee, a friend, he gives her an undiluted picture of just what men want in women.

> Jimmie: "Man is a *very law abiding animal when it comes to decent women.* He wants a decent woman to *stay* decent—and if she *doesn't* he cusses her out for doing the *very* thing he told her was the greatest thing a woman *can* do—*giving him all for love.*"

In a later conversation with Mary, Bridgie, who supplies much ᶠ the humor in the play declares:

> "I tell you this is an awfully *hard age* for a *good* woman to live in. I mean one who wants to have any *fun*. If you've still got the instincts for right

> and wrong that were pounded into you when you were a girl—what are you going to *do* with 'em? And they just get you mixed up—and hold you back—so you're neither one thing nor the other. Neither happy—and bad—nor good and *contented.* You're just *discontentedly decent*—and it doesn't get you *anywhere.*" Later on she says: "After all if people stop to investigate—nobody would ever *marry anybody.*"

Claire Woodruff, wife of the publisher whom Mary loves, is discussing Mary's forthcoming book with her before she knows that her husband has been making love to Mary. To both women what the members of their sex think about Mary's work is more important than what men think.

"Women can't fool women—about *women,*" Claire tells Mary, and when the latter relates the plot of her book, Claire shows her what the wife would probably say to the woman who has come to take her husband away from her.

> "I'd say *of course* something *new* is interesting. *Of course* I look the same old way—and sound the same old way—and eat the same old way—*and so will* you—after a while. I'd say *of course* I can understand his loving you—but are *you prepared to stand up to the job of loving him?*"

His irresistible qualities become exceedingly tedious to live with, while the girl must realize that she can't hold him with just herself.

> "*He* has to have something in *him* that will make him stick to *you.* Nothing else can pull a man and woman through the ghastly job of living together."

When identities are revealed in the play Claire ceases to love her husband, and Mary realizes that she *has* been only "one of the others" of whom Claire told her. Rogers Woodruff tries to win Claire back again but she tells him that at last she has stopped caring for him.

Claire: "You don't even know what I'm talking about.
   You can't conceive that I *could* stop loving you.
   But that's what's happened, Rogers. It's *over*."
Rogers: "Claire—"
Claire: "As completely as if it had never *been*. It
   happened in just one second—I think—when I saw
   what you'd done to *her*."

At the end of the play Mary says that some day she would
have known Claire through Rogers Woodruff, for she suddenly
realizes that whatever fineness there is in him has been brought
out by his wife.   The way the two women spar in the scene between them has made each recognize the fine qualities in the other
and for this reason they despise the man who is true to no decent
code.   He is willing to tamper with the affections not only of
a woman who lacks recognition of social values, but with one
whose sense of fineness and decency is inherent.   This is why
Claire Woodruff tells her husband that she is through.   Until his
affair with Mary Howard, Claire has known that the other women
have been beneath her, that she need feel no personal insult.   But
when she meets Mary and finds that Rogers Woodruff has treated
Mary in the same manner as the others she realizes that he will
do the same thing to her.   She sees that he has absolutely no
sense of fitness whatever.

In these two plays Miss Crothers has given us two distinct
viewpoints which depend upon different sets of circumstances.
In *Let Us Be Gay,* Kitty Brown and her husband have been divorced because of the very same conditions that we met in *Paris
Bound,* but they decide to remarry because each has suffered what
Mary and Jim Hutton manage to avoid in Barry's treatment.
The children in Miss Crothers' play live with their grandmother,
having no real home of their own, while their mother, now in
business, travels.   Bitter regret and a decided lapse in moral
standards follow in the wake of this divorce on the part of both
husband and wife.

However, in *When Ladies Meet* there is nothing for Claire
Woodruff to do but divorce her husband, for in this case he makes
it impossible for her to maintain a decent home.   There is a limit

to the support which society can give to the marriage institution. Claire Woodruff's marriage has become a farce and, still worse, a disgrace to decent society.   To preserve her self-respect and that of her family she naturally takes the only means left.   She is, by her action, raising, not lowering, fundamental social standards.

One of the most recent comedies of manners to take up the question of marriage is A. E. Thomas's *No More Ladies,* produced at the Booth Theatre, New York, January 23rd, 1934.   It is a treatment of a marriage between two young people whom we can describe in no other way than "ultra-modern," and an attempt to adjust them to their new station in life which they never dreamed could be really serious.   One of the most outstanding, and certainly one of the most unfortunate phases of modern life, is the extreme brevity of many marriages in what, for lack of a better name, is known as the "world of society."   With plenty of money at their command a divorce means no hardship whatever, but is an open gate to freedom and pleasure.   This condition has become so prevalent that the real meaning of marriage is totally lost to many people who regard it as a pastime to be discarded when they become bored with each other.   In Thomas' play nothing could be in more violent contrast to the old-fashioned proposal of marriage than the agreement of Marcia Townsend and Sherry Warren to make an attempt at marriage.

> Marcia : "I'll tell you one thing, it's going to be the most marvelous party in the world; or it's going to be hell.   So watch out!"
> Sherry : "I've always wondered if there was really a hell."
> Marcia : "Well, my lad, you'll have a sporting chance to find out."
> Sherry; pulls her up: "Well, we're off."
> Marcia : "Just a moment, my good man.   Let's get this straight."
> Sherry : "Right-ho!"
> Marcia : "We're a pair of fools."
> Sherry : "Imbecile."
> Marcia : "We haven't a chance."
> Sherry : "Not an earthly."
> Marcia : "It's bound to be the most heart-rending flop."
> Sherry : "Hideous!"

Marcia: "We can't miss—"
Sherry: "Horse breaks down at post."
Marcia: "So we bet on him just the same."
Sherry: "Every dollar we've got."
Marcia: "Well then. Let's go."

At this conclusion they embrace, when suddenly into the room bursts Fanny, the very, very modern grandmother who warns them both, with the exclamation, "My God! The ship's afire!" And indeed she has spoken truly. After one year of being harnessed Sherry has an affair and Marcia discovers to her surprise and annoyance that she is thoroughly aroused. Sherry's apology does little to soothe her rage and it is not until after she has made him sufficiently jealous and wretched that the play closes on what we at least hope is a permanent reconciliation.

On the whole it is evident that in nearly every play we have discussed which deals with married relations, preservation of marriage and the home is upheld. *Episode* and *When Ladies Meet* are the outstanding exceptions for in both of these plays divorce alone can save the self-respect of the characters. When Eve Ryesdale tells her husband that he will spend the rest of his life forgiving her, she is exactly right, for he is the kind of man who could never feel the same toward her again. He would never let her forget what she had done. Any real happiness in their marriage is not impossible. This same fact is true of *When Ladies Meet* for there is nothing left of the marriage between Rogers and Claire Woodruff. He has destroyed every vestige of the essential laws and codes upon which marriage is based. In both of these plays the futility of continuing an impossible marriage is as apparent as the futility of divorce is in plays like *Let Us Be Gay* and *Paris Bound*.

F.   THE INTERRELATIONS BETWEEN SOCIETY AND BUSINESS AND PUBLIC LIFE

Among the earliest plays to deal with the strong influence that business has had upon social life were Mrs. Mowatt's *Fashion*

(1845), Mrs. Bateman's *Self* (1856), and *The Golden Calf* (1857). It was during the middle of the century when the industrial revolution gained momentum that the great changes in society which have been going on ever since, first began to be noticeable. There was a tremendous growth in the urban population of the country while side by side with the increase of wealth came the opportunity for education and leisure for many who had never had advantages before. Consequently there are two marked phases which developed along with the increasingly strong bond between society and business. In the first place, there was the spectacle of the social climber, and secondly, there was the disrupting influence upon home life of the exclusive devotion to business on the part of the husband.

When, in 1845, Mrs. Mowatt's *Fashion* was produced it created a sensation. Severe critic though he was, Edgar Allan Poe gave the play the credit due it and recognized its merits. Mrs. Tiffany, who evidences the parvenu's lack of understanding of real social values, is a sheer delight from beginning to end. Her attempts to speak French, to hold what she supposes to be a salon in the French manner and her determined efforts to walk gracefully and sit down with a sweeping gesture of ease are a constant source of amusement. Mrs. Mowatt has caricatured her, but even at that she remains rather human and not just a type. Unfortunately, Mrs. Tiffany's efforts to break into circles for which she is not fitted bring her husband to the verge of bankruptcy and this is a theme which we find running through three of the plays that we shall next discuss. Apparently, there was a perfect epidemic of bankrupts or we should hardly find it reflected in the drama so frequently in so short a period. Mrs. Tiffany has spent money to her heart's content but she is far from being contented, for her object now is not only to gain the top of the ladder but to marry her daughter off to a Count Jolimaître. He is a great find as Mrs. Tiffany thinks he is French. She exudes politeness and rapturous joy when he arrives at her salon. Behind the scenes, however, trouble brews, for Mr. Snobson, Tiffany's business partner, has promised to save his associate from bankruptcy if he may marry

Seraphina Tiffany. He calls to see Seraphina, whereupon Mrs. Tiffany gathers her dignity about her and replies:

> "Permit me to inform you, Mr. Snobson, that a French mother never leaves her daughter alone with a young man—she knows your sex too well for that."
>
> Snobson: "Very *dis*obliging of her—but as we're none French—"
>
> Mrs. Tiffany: "You have yet to learn, Mr. Snobson, that the American *eelight*—the aristocracy—the *how-ton* —as a matter of conscience, scrupulously follow the foreign fashions."

Thus does Mrs. Tiffany murder the French language for the sake of being fashionable and she represents a large class of new rich which was springing up like mushrooms during this period of our history. There is an excellent contrast drawn between Mrs. Tiffany and Gertrude, a governess, who is a gentlewoman. Her quiet, reserved manner makes the family with whom she lives seem all the more ostentatious and vulgar. It is an excellent illustration of the contrast between the social climber who must be in the limelight constantly and the person who doesn't consider making a display. Gertrude's innate self-respect and Mrs. Tiffany's lack of any draws a sharp line of distinction between the two women.

Self, by Mrs. Sidney Bateman, produced in 1856, is a play on the same pattern as *Fashion* but is much inferior to it both in characterization and dialogue. It is a very artificial play and except for the fact that it reflects a certain phase of society during the middle of the century it could hardly hold our interest. Mrs. Apex is another Mrs. Tiffany to whom money and fashion are everything. Through superficial accomplishments she pretends to be a patron of the arts, but of course, in reality knows nothing. Her son, Charles, is the typical high flyer of his day who loses large sums of money through gambling. Mr. Apex is the long suffering husband who loses everything through his wife's extravagance. A crash in the stock market which occurred around this time is mentioned in the play and there is frequent reference to the general rush for money which the increase in business was bringing about.   One gets no glimpse of the society into which Mrs. Apex is struggling to make her way and this is one of the peculiarities of the social satires of this period which has been noted before.   Only here and there in these plays does one meet with a character who is not a climber.

The Golden Calf: or *Marriage à la Mode,* also by Mrs. Bateman, produced in St. Louis, 1857, while essentially an international contrast, portrays a very crude and vulgar American, Crassus Stearine, Esq., who goes to Europe and tries to buy his daughter a position in society.   She is just as bad as her father for, like him; she is still impressed with their great wealth, so newly acquired, and both she and her father speak constantly of it.   He feels that anything can be gotten if you have the money to pay for it and is totally unable to make any distinction between people.   The play ends with a moral which warns us not to fall down in worship of the mighty dollar, when one of the characters says:

> ". . . But let us never forget that social worship of the Golden Calf, mammon, is paying to that emblem of past barbarism a reverence only due to the more worthy shrines of Genius, Honor, Truth and Virtue."

Crassus Stearine, Esq., with his love of money and his consideration of everything in life from a mercenary standpoint, exemplifies one type of American who was emerging from the business boom during the eighteen fifties.

The first social comedy which dealt seriously with the disastrous effects that the strain of modern business so often has upon the home was Bronson Howard's *Young Mrs. Winthrop* (1882). Constance and Douglas Winthrop have become almost strangers to each other largely because of the high tension which modern life imposes upon them.   Douglas is completely occupied with business while his wife, as a result, has turned more and more to a social life for diversion.   Unlike the satires that preceded it, *Young Mrs. Winthrop* is a straight-forward presentation of life, dealing with one of its major problems.   The decades which followed the Civil War witnessed another tremendous industrial development, and one which brought about great differences in society. This was the "Gilded Age" in American history, when the large cities were flooded with new rich families who had made their money elsewhere and now entered metropolitan life with the hope of becoming social leaders. They employed European tutors to give them the polish they lacked, purchased rare art objects and bought their way into society. The famous "four hundred" originated during this period and lasted until the end of the century, when the tide of "outsiders" became so great that it broke down the barriers. A display of wealth never before seen in this country was the occasion of the Bradley Martin's ball in 1897, when they turned the Waldorf Astoria into a replica of Versailles. Unhappily, 1897 was a depression year and so great was the criticism that the Martins had to flee to Europe.[6]

This was the age, too, when married women as well as single ones were entering the business world in large numbers. They were independent as they had never been before, many of them owning property and the logical sequence of this change in woman's status was a change in her way of thinking. If she chose, she obtained a divorce without being in disgrace for doing so. In Howard's play, Constance and Douglas Winthrop agree to part since they are no longer congenial—a move which would not have been considered by either one of them thirty years before—but by this time a woman like Constance Winthrop could separate from her husband and still maintain her position in society. Furthermore, throughout the play she comes and goes as she pleases which reveals a great difference from the woman who in former times had either to depend upon her husband to go out with her or to stay at home. To counterbalance the serious theme of the play Howard introduces Mrs. Chetwyn, a "grass widow," who constantly mixes the names of her husbands, past, present and future. Her confusion and her flippant manner are extremely humorous and in many ways she points forward to the same type of character we meet in present day plays, like Bridget in Rachel Crothers' *When Ladies Meet*. *Young Mrs. Winthrop* contains

---

[6] Beard, *The Rise of American Civilization*, part II, pp. 392-393.

some very fine character studies and is the first American comedy, except *The Contrast* that preserved the tone and atmosphere of true social comedy from beginning to end.   By making an honest presentation of a current problem with which society is faced, instead of resorting to satire, Howard took a great step forward.

In 1887 *The Henrietta* opened at the Union Square Theatre and proved a tremendous success.   It is not so strictly social comedy as *Young Mrs. Winthrop* for its main theme centers around the dealings on the Stock Exchange and it is shot through with biting satire.   In the earlier play the business world remained more in the background, as an outside force, the effects of which upon the lives of the Winthrops and upon society in general Howard stressed.   But in *The Henrietta* we see at first hand the business world in operation.   The unscrupulous methods of much of the trading on the Exchange come to light, and yet Howard takes a fair viewpoint when he shows that a man conducts himself in business as he has been taught by the example of other men.   He simply knows no other way, and when his actions ruin someone else it is not because he has acted from personal prejudice, but in his own interests without thinking of the other person at all. In general, however, the play is a satire on the cold, hard methods of both business and social life, for the two cannot be separated. There is an excellent contrast between a younger son who holds business in contempt and his elder brother and father whose lives are wrapped up in the perpetual fever of the financial world.   The interrelations between society and business provided one of the main subjects of interest for Howard and he has portrayed this particular phase of life with skill and insight.

A character in de Mille's and Belasco's *Charity Ball* (1889), resembles the elder brother in Howard's *The Henrietta* for he is devoting himself to the gain of wealth to the exclusion of every finer instinct in him.   In Howard's play the man dies from over-strain, but in *The Charity Ball* his brother and the woman he loves save him.   The calamitous effect upon an individual of abandoning himself completely to the obsession of reaching the summit of business success, regardless of those around him, is very well shown in both plays, although Howard has given a more real and credible presentation.

At the turn of the century we find Clyde Fitch taking up this same theme. *A Modern Match* (1892), centers around a woman who has married for money and who leaves her husband when he is financially ruined. Ten years later she returns for her daughter's wedding but is refused admittance. The contrast between her and another woman who never fails her husband is well drawn. The play has many of Fitch's characteristic touches and expressions such as "Fashionable people, like the good, die young." Primarily a domestic comedy, *A Modern Match* gives one a good picture of the turbulence of modern life which makes it so difficult for people to find the leisure necessary to enjoy life together. Business, social life, the continual scramble for money to keep up with someone else, and the eternal search for diversion are all present in this play. Fitch shows how little regard the woman who leaves her husband has for anything really fine. The standards she ought to uphold she abandons for false ones. She is an example of the woman who measures happiness only in the light of money and when there is no more money she is either unwilling or unable to face life without it. She assumes that other people's respect for her depends upon superficial appearances, not upon character or the qualities of a gentlewoman.

The Climbers, produced in 1901, is one of the best examples of social climbing that we have in American drama. The opening scene is the Hunters' drawing room just after Mr. Hunter's funeral. His widow is in ecstasy over the splendid spectacle that the funeral has been and exclaims to her daughters: "My dears, it was a great success! Everybody was there!" The outburst immediately establishes Mrs. Hunter for what she is; a vain, ignorant woman but one who is sharp where her own welfare is concerned. An unusually fine contrast between her and her sister-in-law, Ruth Hunter, who is a cultured, well-bred woman, shows Fitch's remarkable ability in characterization. The three daughters are excellently drawn, also, two of them being very fine. Jessica wishes to go to work when she finds that her father has left no money. The different viewpoints about women entering business at that period come up in conversation. Unlike the present day, the matter needed much consideration, for the feeling that a certain stigma was attached to the woman in business had not died out by any means. Mrs. Hunter, needless to say, is aghast over the idea, while Jessica and Blanche take the opposite stand.

At times Mrs. Hunter becomes a Mrs. Malaprop of a distinct type. She remarries, and when she advises Blanche to get a divorce and remarry and Blanche replies that her own case is not analagous to hers, Mrs. Hunter exclaims: "Not what? You needn't fling any innuendoes at Mr. Trotter." Divorce, she declares, is made for woman and when Ruth Hunter asks whether polygamy is made for man, she answers: "I don't know anything about politics."

The dialogue gives us an accurate and surprisingly complete picture of social life with its everchanging vogues and conventions. Fitch is often described as a clever, entertaining playwright, but one who seldom goes below the surface. However, when one stops to consider critically the plays of Clyde Fitch, he will find that the playwright has done far more than just scratch the surface, but because of the ease with which he expresses his ideas in the sparkling dialogue that he employs, the critic at first glance fails to catch what is frequently a fundamental truth, or perhaps he misses the irony which at times cuts very deeply indeed.

The Climbers shows not only the complete ruin financially of families overnight when a market crash occurs, but there is a fine study of the disintegration of a man's character when he is possessed with the fever of speculation. In this particular case, he embezzles, loses his wife's love as a result of it, and finally commits suicide. The whole scene of New York society forms the background of this play with the individual struggles that go on to maintain a position in the sun. Probably one of the most delightful touches in the play is Mrs. Hunter's explanation to her children of the reason she thinks society has snubbed her. She refers to her husband's position socially and then proceeds to say: "I consider my family was just as good as his, only we were *Presbyterians.*" This remark evidences the superiority that the Episcopal element has always maintained for itself from the very earliest period in our history down to the present day. The members of this particular denomination have always regarded themselves as the very pillars of the "old order" in society and will invariably create the impression that to be anything but an Episcopalian is a misfortune not to be taken lightly.   Naturally, Mrs. Hunter is not beyond the pale because of her being Presbyterian, but because she *is* and always *has* been hopeless socially, and she is uncomfortably aware of the fact but must give what she trusts will be a satisfactory explanation.   As we have noted before, Clyde Fitch apparently never missed anything, and his observance of the superiority that one religious denomination will assume over another is typical of him.

In one other play of Fitch's, we again have the financial world as a background.   *Her Own Way* (1903), centers around a woman steadfast in her love in spite of forces that work against her faith.   The power of money to make or break a person—here it is the latter—is an important motive in the play while the theme of social climbing again enters into the plot.   Speculation at its worst is brought out, but in a different light from that in either Howard's *Henrietta* or in *The Climbers,* for here malice is the underlying reason for one person ruining another.   The play lacks the interest that *The Climbers* contains and the characters seem more conventional and remote.

Just as absorption in business can have an adverse influence upon the institution of the family, so can a public career.   A play which shows how vocations of this kind can raise a barrier between members of a family is James Forbes' *The Famous Mrs. Fair.*   Here we see a woman so completely engrossed in public life that her family goes to pieces as a result.

The play, produced in 1919, is a powerful study of a woman, Nancy Fair, who has won widespread fame for her work overseas during the World War and who, upon coming home, finds her two children grown into maturity and her husband Jeffrey filling in his lonely hours with a young widow.   However, his interest in this woman has not become serious, for like the rest of the family, he has been living for the time when Nancy will be home. But, instead of settling down with her family, she makes arrangements for a series of lecture tours and travels constantly.   Finally, her daughter's affair with Gillette, Nancy's promoter and publicity man, brings her to her senses. Furthermore, Jeffrey's association with the other woman has developed into an affair which threatens to break up his marriage completely.

The question arises as to whether Nancy, through her neglect, or Jeffrey, because of his affair, has done the greater wrong. His disappointment when she plainly shows that she does not intend to stay at home and the disillusionment that the whole family feels seem to place more blame upon her. However, in the eyes of conventional society, Jeffrey has broken one of the strict codes which must be preserved. Nancy Fair condemns her husband without reservation when she first learns of his unfaithfulness, but gradually she realizes her own contribution to the situation and the play closes upon a note of reconciliation.

The discontent of the women who belong to Nancy's war unit when they face comparative idleness after so much activity, is amusingly shown in one instance when one of them says that she has taken to card-indexing her hens in order to pass the time. However, the terrible restlessness on the part of both the men and women who returned from the war was only natural after their being keyed up to the pitch of the frantic life around them. Much of the post-war madness was a direct result of not being able to stand idleness, and in his play Forbes has given a very sympathetic and understanding treatment of this situation. If people couldn't use up their energy by finding something useful to do, they turned to dissipation, but Nancy Fair's active public career, while possibly of some use, destroys what is of the greatest value not only in her own life but in that of her husband and children. Needless to say, a general condition of this kind would soon reduce society to a hopeless state, one in which there would be little regard for any standards or laws whatever.

It is interesting to note how the social comedies which reflect the interrelations between business and public life, with society, follow closely the development of American life. The very early comedies do not deal with this phase because life in the early years of the United States was not nearly so complicated as it is today. When the industrial revolution spread over this country during the middle of the nineteenth century, we have seen how the plays of that period immediately reflected the rush for money; how people spent more than they made in order to keep up with someone else, or to break into circles from which they were previously barred.

In the plays of Howard, especially *Young Mrs. Winthrop,* we have seen the disastrous effect upon the home of a man's absorption in business.   In *The Henrietta,* the unscrupulous aspect of Wall Street trading comes before us.   Not only does Howard show the bitter rivalry between financial firms but he studies the effect upon the individual owing to the stress of this particular vocation.   This same theme runs through the plays of Clyde Fitch that we have just discussed.   Both of these dramatists present this aspect of business from the same viewpoint.   Each has given us a portrait of an individual whose character becomes undermined because of his obsession to reach the pinnacle of financial success through speculation.

In James Forbes' *The Famous Mrs. Fair,* it is a woman whose preoccupation with a public career causes her to forget her family. This play reflects the complete independence that has come to women and is a far cry from the early comedies.

Generally, this phase of American social comedy is an accurate picture of the increasing complexity in American life.   The growing independence on the part of women, the growing absorption on the part of men in business which affects their home life are all clearly portrayed by American playwrights.

G.   THE CONFLICT BETWEEN SOCIETY AND LOVE

There has always been an unspoken conflict between society and love.   Forces which people sense but cannot definitely grasp have had a certain restraining influence upon lovers.   Sometimes the stress of social life is so strong that love between two people is ruined; prejudices stand in the way and it is up to the individuals to rise above these forces and triumph over them.

One of the best illustrations we have of two people in conventional society who are very much in love but who are bound to observe propriety to the letter, is William Dean Howells' *Five O'clock Tea* (1889), which has already been discussed at some length.   Not for worlds would Mrs. Somers display the fact that she loves Willis Campbell although his courtship has been going on for a long time.   Both of them know, of course, that she will accept him when she feels satisfied that she has kept him waiting a proper length of time.   This, in Campbell's estimation, she has done and to settle her he decides to leave her tea just as Mrs. Curwen, whom Mrs. Somers secretly detests, is going.   This is most uncomfortable for Mrs. Somers and delightful for Mrs. Curwen, who sees through the situation and tells Campbell to stay, which of course he does.   Finally, after leaving the room in a state of confusion, which reduces her to tears, Mrs. Somers reappears before her guests ready to announce the engagement. Howells' description of her entrance into the room is a perfect classic as a revelation of human nature and good-humored satire. She 'radiantly reappears.'   "She has hidden the traces of her tears from everyone but the ladies, by a light application of powder, and she knows that they all know she has been crying and this makes her a little more smiling."

The clever counter-play on the part of Amy Somers and Willis Campbell, the sophisticated skirmishes between them, and the whole situation laid against a background of a society that based life upon the recognition of every social convention to the letter, renders *Five O'clock Tea* one of the most brilliant and perfect examples of the comedy of manners in American drama.

A charming one act play, *Old Love Letters* (1878), by Bronson Howard in which the social scene operates to clever advantage, reveals the revival of an old love between two people.   Mrs. Florence Brownlee, a widow of about thirty, and the Honorable Edward Warburton have not seen each other since they quarreled thirteen years before.   Warburton has come to return a packet of letters Mrs. Brownlee had written to him and she is about to return his, but their love for each other flames up anew.   We know that Mrs. Brownlee has the letters with her but rather than let Warburton know such a thing, she sends her maid for them. In spite of the brevity of the play the conversation between the two characters reveals for us an almost complete picture of the years that have intervened since their quarrel. We gather that Mrs. Brownlee has had a quiet, agreeable life married to a man years older than she, whom she admired but with whom she was never in love. Warburton has had a successful career but both have missed real happiness. The social atmosphere of the world in which they move permeates the play and lends to it an air of quiet dignity and restraint which raises it to a level of distinction. Both characters instinctively have to overcome a certain pride which is natural to them and both feel called upon to suppress the emotion which they feel. This conflict within ourselves results directly from the environment and atmosphere around us and we cannot free ourselves from it without overstepping the social codes which guide our lives.

Clyde Fitch's *The Stubbornness of Geraldine,* produced in 1902, shows a girl fighting for her rights in the face of strong opposition. Geraldine Lang is an American girl who has fallen in love with a Hungarian count while on board ship returning from Europe. At first, both of her foster parents and friends accept him but shortly rumors of business scandals as well as of a sordid love affair reach their ears and they try to persuade the girl not to see him any more. However, she knows intuitively that he is a gentleman and later a case of mistaken identity proves her to be right. It is this confidence in Geraldine in her lover that makes the play important. She is too fine a person not to be able to detect a serious flaw in his character. Were he unfit to associate with decent, respectable people, the girl would recognize the fact. It is this essential understanding on her part that makes her an interesting character, for only once does she show a momentary hesitation. Her conflict lies not within herself in this case, but with the whole force of society which is ready to pounce upon an individual and destroy him. Under the circumstances presented in this play, the individual cannot, for certain reasons, speak to clear himself but must depend upon the faith of those around him until the opportunity arrives. The play reveals how quickly and easily a really fine love between two people can be destroyed unless they have character enough to defy the forces that operate against them.

A light touch in the play lies in the bridge lessons that four New York women are taking from an expert instructor whom they drive to distraction. After a minute or two of playing they launch forth upon a sea of gossip and forget completely the cards they hold. The satire, in this case against the woman who is bound to take up whatever is popular but hates to exert herself in order to master it, is typical of Fitch, who never missed seeing whatever happened to be going on, and who always saw the humorous angle of it.

Philip Barry's *Holiday* again illustrates this timeless conflict between society and love and the conflicts that arise in the individuals themselves. The love which has sprung up between Johnny Case and Linda Seton after Linda's sister Julia has shown that she cares more for stuffy security than she does for Johnny, is a love upon which conventional society always frowns. To begin with, society cannot bear to have people snap their fingers at it and escape from its smothering protection to freedom. Certainly anyone who saw *Holiday* must have had one of those exhilarating moments not common in life when in the final scene Linda breaks down the barriers and seizes life whole. At that, she is doing nothing to lower either hers or anybody else's standards, nor is she harming anyone. She is merely escaping from an intolerable weight of social convention which each generation of Setons has piled up more crushingly, escaping from the "tradition" of her family of which she has been reminded so often. She is marrying the man she loves in spite of society and she leaves behind her a deflated family pride. In this play the Seton clan has no objections to Johnny as an individual, for he disarms them all, even Edward Seton, the father, for a brief time, but they do object to what *they* consider an almost insane plan for the future.

The plays in this particular phase of American social comedy are fewer in number because the playwrights have generally centered their attention upon a more tangible problem. There is, of course, a love theme through practically every play we have discussed but it is not the especial point upon which the playwright has laid emphasis. This is probably owing to the desire on the part of American audiences for a more substantial theme. The pure comedy of manners has never been as popular in this country as it is in England and on the Continent.   Plays like *Five O'clock Tea, Old Love Letters* and *The Stubbornness of Geraldine* are charming and entertaining but they do not have the same importance that plays with a more serious thesis possess.   Their appeal is limited to a smaller group of people.

CHAPTER III

THE TYPES OF CHARACTERS SOCIAL COMEDY HAS DEVELOPED

There are certain types of characters indigenous to every field of the drama. Social comedy has developed an interesting and widely divergent number of individuals who contribute their share in the formation of society. They are the people whom we see every day around us, whom we censure or praise according to their attitude and conduct. Some of them belong to a generation that has passed, some link the generations together, while still others foreshadow the immediate future. Many of them uphold and respect the standards which govern their lives while there are others who break down these standards whenever they can.

Let us begin first of all with a character who respects the codes by which he lives, namely, the gentleman. He is a person who, first of all, never changes essentially. His style of dress may be different at different periods, he may be more formal in one age of history than in another, but fundamentally he is the same. Our very first comedy, *The Contrast,* contains just such a man in the person of Colonel Manly. Throughout the play he shows not only in his conduct and conversation the highest ideals that an individual can have but also typifies the kind of man upon whom society can depend to maintain its highest standards. To us today, Colonel Manly may seem too formal and stiff in his manner, too serious in his outlook upon life, but no one can deny him the title of "gentleman," for his sense of honor and chivalry are elemental characteristics. He stands for the unaffected, frank but courteous man, to whom any sort of sham or deception is hateful.

More than a century later Clyde Fitch drew the portrait of a gentleman in the character of Beau Brummell, a dandy of the early nineteenth century. In contrast to Manly who cared very little for dress, Beau is almost a fanatic on this subject. Not the

131

slightest detail does he overlook, while his manner is affected, to conform with the fashion of the day. He is not the same type of man as Colonel Manly and yet beneath his polished, affected manner, he possesses, in the play, the same sterling qualities of character—chivalry, a sense of honor and an unswerving devotion to his ideals. Beau cares for appearances, Manly does not, but both are fundamentally fine and abide by their ideals.

An example of the gentleman of the late nineteenth century is John Austin in Clyde Fitch's *The Girl with the Green Eyes*. He seems at first an average man but as the play progresses we become more and more aware of his unusually fine character. Without a trace of jealousy himself, he endures his wife's unreasonable jealousy with admirable patience. Even in the scene when he can stand Jinny's false accusations no longer and leaves her, he still maintains his dignity and restraint. His essential fineness is shown by his not revealing to her the fact that her brother is a bigamist. He could tell her this and save himself the torture he suffers from her jealous nature but he refuses to tell her because of her love for her brother. Throughout the play Austin's unselfish nature impresses itself upon us and the sacrifice he makes to conceal a painful truth from his wife makes him an admirable figure.

When we turn now to the gentleman of contemporary times we meet Charles Lingard of Rachel Crothers' *As Husbands Go*. Here is a self-effacing man, one who goes on his quiet way, devoted to his wife, happy in his home, respected by his friends. As we have already seen, his fine character and love are reflected in his wife, and have made her the perfect being she *seems*. Charles Lingard is one of thousands of men who are admired and beloved by their friends but who otherwise pass unnoticed in life. He is the type of gentleman whose fineness immediately radiates to those around him, but one who is totally unconscious of his own presence. Unlike Beau Brummell, who is aware of his every movement, Charles Lingard is unassuming and never for a moment considers the effect of his presence.

In these portraits we have representative gentlemen of several different periods in history. One is an Englishman but he is typical of the dandy in Colonial America as well. Colonel Manly, John Austin and Charles Lingard are thoroughly American, and in their complete naturalness and unassuming manner combined with a frankness and a recognition of the finest ideals, are representative of the highest type of gentleman.

When we turn now to the opposite sex and choose a representative gentlewoman we think at once of Gertrude in Mrs. Mowatt's *Fashion,* of Amy Somers in Howells' comedies and of Claire Woodruff in Rachel Crothers' *When Ladies Meet.* There is less of a contrast between these three women than there is between the gentlemen discussed.

Gertrude, in *Fashion,* is, to be sure, of a more retiring nature than either of the other two, because she belonged to an age when this quality in a woman was expected. The contrast between her and the people around her is excellently drawn, as we have already seen, for she is a person who dislikes any sort of public display because of its obvious vulgarity. Despite the fact that she is a governess and therefore dependent upon other people for her support she maintains a spirit of independence and self assurance which none of her associates possesses. It is this which distinguishes her from the other characters.

Amy Somers, in Howells' plays, who later becomes Mrs. Willis Campbell, is an excellent character to illustrate the gentlewoman of the latter part of the nineteenth century. She is bound by her observance of the conventions to bow to the artificialities of her day but there is about her a keenness and cleverness that makes her an outstanding figure. One always feels that she sees through everyone else and that she is equal to any situation, however trying. Brilliant, charming and possessed of an assurance that is unshakeable, she looms above the other women around her. She is what is known as a "social leader," a woman whom all other women admire and envy. Thoroughly feminine but rather despising the weaknesses of her sex, she is one of the finest character creations in American drama.

For a portrayal of the contemporary gentlewoman we turn to Claire Woodruff in Rachel Crothers' *When Ladies Meet.* Claire Woodruff has met with an admirable dignity and self restraint the most terrible humiliation that can come to one of her sex—the unfaithfulness of her husband. She has been able to do this because she loves him deeply and because, until the affair which withers her love, she feels that the women with whom her husband has been associating, are beneath her. Miss Crothers has drawn a portrait of a woman whose self-respect, whose high ideals in life, and whose loyalty are an inherent part of her character. Never for a moment does she lose her poise, her self-control and never has she stooped to even so much as question her husband, whose habits she knows only too well. When, in the end, she sees him for what he really is; when she realizes that he has as little regard for the feelings of another gentlewoman as for women with no morals, she still retains her self-possession and the restraint which befits her. In her conversation, she is, to be sure, more outspoken than the Victorian woman, but this simply reveals the difference between the generations. These three women, Gertrude, Amy Somers (Campbell) and Claire Woodruff are all typical of the age in which they live. All three are impeccable in their conduct; all three are representative of the finest type of American gentlewoman.

There are in several plays young girls typical of the age in which they live. Charlotte Manly, in *The Contrast,* is a perfect picture of the coquette of her day in her desire to live to please the men. Vain, a little foolish, but gifted with a sprightly sense of humor and a generous spirit, she is the belle of the late eighteenth century. In many ways Charlotte seems more modern than Geraldine Lang in Fitch's *The Stubbornness of Geraldine,* in spite of the fact that Fitch's play was produced over a hundred years later. The difference, however, lies in their characters for Charlotte is very much a flirt while Geraldine is a more stable person. Fitch's heroine possesses a frank, easy manner that is very charming and winsome. She has an unassuming air of self-possession and assurance that at once stamp her as a girl whose position is unquestioned.

For the girl of the twentieth century we may turn to Philip Barry's *You and I.* Veronica (Ronny) Duane is typical of the cultured, self reliant girl of today. The contrast between her and the two girls already discussed lies mainly in the new freedom that women now possess. As we have already pointed out, Ronny does not need to depend upon marriage for her career but is free to enter the world of business. A choice of this kind was not open to Charlotte Manly or to Geraldine Lang, although women were beginning to enter public life to a certain extent in Fitch's time. All three of these girls are typical of the young gentle-woman of their respective times.

In selecting a young boy we may choose Sydney Osbert from James Nelson Barker's *Tears and Smiles* for he is an example of a young man whose principles will not let him stoop to anything beneath his station in life. He is a rather conventional type of character who appeared in the very early plays but he illustrates the playwright's ideal of a young American.

For a boy of the late nineteenth century there is Benny Demaresq in Augustin Daly's *Railroad of Love*. He seems more natural and real than Sydney Osbert and is typical of his age. He possesses a certain shyness and is quiet in his manner. His attitude toward his elders is quite different from Roderick Maitland in Philip Barry's *You and I*. Roderick, or "Ricky," exemplifies the assurance of today's younger generation in making its own decisions. A certain disarming flippancy which never becomes rudeness, a frank, open manner and an innate restraint of his emotions reveal him as the young gentleman of today. He is the kind of person upon whom society can depend for maintaining its highest standards. When we turn to the next type of character that social comedy has developed we find a totally different sort of person from those whom we have discussed.

The adventuress is present in many kinds of drama but in social comedy she is particularly important because she is one of the characters who will smash the social laws when she can. Vida Phillimore in Langdon Mitchell's *New York Idea,* a divorcée, is a woman who is bored with her existence and who is ready for excitement. Her carefully laid plans to ensnare John Karslake, divorced husband of Cynthia, are typical of a woman of her kind. When she fails to get him she calmly turns to Sir Wilfrid Cates-

Darby, the Englishman, for she has few scruples and almost no feeling.

Caroline Knollys in Louis K. Anspacher's *Unchastened Woman* is a better example of the adventuress for she is without any real sense of decency whatever. She knows the laws by which she must live and she is clever enough never to break the most essential one. But she is a woman to whom fine feelings are unknown, a woman who mocks every code by which society must stand or fall. Completely unmoral, she is never immoral. She lives merely for herself and if in her trifling with the affections of men she undermines their characters or destroys their homes she is not in the least disturbed by it. It is all a part of her game. This type of woman is always at war with society, and in the final analysis she loses her fight against the stronger and more powerful forces of decency and essential fitness.

Another figure unpopular in society, and yet the product of social conventions, is the snob. In the early social comedies he was nearly always present and generally he was not only a snob, but was an impostor as well. Dimple, in *The Contrast;* Fluttermore, in *Tears and Smiles* and Worthnought in Samuel Low's *Politician Outwitted* are examples of the young fops who scorned their own country and preferred European customs. Of course, at the end of each play they turn out to be either blackguards or as in the case of a later play, *Fashion,* impostors. The reason for this character's presence was the opportunity for contrasting him with fine examples of American men and women. The snob was little more than a foil, a conventional stage character who served a special purpose.

Today we often find that the worst snob is the successful business man, or one who has inherited through several generations financial and social security. This is true of Edward Seton in Philip Barry's *Holiday* for never could we find a more perfectly self satisfied individual or one who held himself more aloof from the common herd. As his daughter Linda says to Johnny Case when the latter speaks of owning some shares of common stock— "Don't mention the word 'common'." Edward Seton is one of those men, however, whom society regards as a pillar, for he will uphold to his dying day every convention and tradition upon which the class to which he belongs is founded. Anyone outside of his immediate circle who shows an inclination to break down a few traditions, or who mocks, instead of reveres, convention, is simply an outcast unworthy of the barest notice.

Another type of snob is the social climber, for a climber feels that he must assume an aloof attitude in order to make a pretense of drawing distinctions. The social climber has ever been a source of amusement and annoyance. From time immemorial there have been social climbers, and so long as the human race continues they will form a large part of it. In a comparatively new country like the United States where there has been rapid business and financial growth it is natural that the social climber occupies a conspicuous place in society. This is obvious from the dramas which center around the theme of social climbing. One of the characters in American drama typical of this particular individual is Mrs. Tiffany in Mrs. Mowatt's *Fashion*. We have already met Mrs. Tiffany with her French ways and her lavish expenditures. Mrs. Mowatt exaggerates her but she belongs none the less to a very definite species of the human race. However, Mrs. Tiffany is not clever enough to avoid being a laughing stock but must go to extremes in making a grand spectacle of herself for she feels that this is necessary in order to get anywhere.

In the next decade Mrs. Bateman's play *Self* (1856) satirized the social climber, but Mrs. Apex, a character fashioned after Mrs. Tiffany, is not nearly so good a creation. However, she serves to prove that there was a mad scramble on the part of many new rich families to gain a social position.

With Clyde Fitch's play *The Climbers* we have a much better picture of that phase of life. Mrs. Hunter is a very real person indeed. There is no caricature in her case. She stands before us as an ignorant but shrewd woman. It takes very little to make her forget the superficial polish she has acquired and become the crude woman she really is. Her daughter, Blanche, is very fine but is married to Jack Sterling, another type of climber. His obsession to reach the top in the financial world and become a "prince" leads him to dishonesty.

Several other characters, Miss Godesby, Miss Sillerton and Trotter belong to an unscrupulous element which skirts the edge of society. They arrive to buy new clothes belonging to Mrs. Hunter and her daughters which the latter cannot wear because of Mr. Hunter's death. The following conversation takes place while they are waiting for the Hunters to appear.

> Trotter: "Say! the youngest daughter is a good looker— very classy."
> Miss Sillerton: "That's the one we told you about, the one we want you to marry."
> Miss Godesby: "Yes, with your money and her cleverness, she'll rubber neck you into the smartest push in town!"
> Trotter: "You've promised I shall know the whole classy lot before spring."
> Miss Godesby: "So you will if you do as we tell you. But you mustn't let society see that you *know* you're getting in; nothing pleases society so much as to think you're a blatant idiot. It makes everybody feel you're their equal—that's why you get in."

Need any more be said about the climber? It would be an impertinence.

Very early in social comedy we find a character who is always allowed a certain freedom not found in the others. This is the widow. From the Widow Freegrace in *Tears and Smiles* down to "Bridgie" in *When Ladies Meet* the widow seems to sail in and out of plays with a free manner and a free tongue. She is generally endowed with an amazing flow of conversation and while much of it is nonsense there is always a great deal of very sane philosophy. Sometimes this philosophy is rattled off in a nonsensical manner so that unless our ears are open we shall miss the meaning.

The Widow Freegrace in Barker's *Tears and Smiles* is a strikingly modern sort of person. She has little regard for stuffy convention and is the person to whom the young lovers go in their difficulties. It is she who aids Louisa Campdon and Sydney Osbert to overcome the obstacles that beset their path to the altar together.   She is the most attractive character in the play because she is very much alive and stands in awe of no one.   She does as she pleases and is amused if criticised.   A certain aura of worldliness always seems to envelop the character of the widow for in every play in which she appears she fills the role of an oracle.   Whether or not the other characters turn to her for advice she showers it upon them from the point of view of her own experience.   Furthermore, she generally takes the male sex with a grain of salt, or wishes people to think she does.

Mrs. Chetwyn in Bronson Howard's *Young Mrs. Winthrop* is an example of the widow who cannot even keep the names of her husbands straight.   She has just decided to remarry one of her former husbands and continually gets his name mixed with another.   She is a chatterbox but she serves to reveal the modern viewpoint toward divorce and points forward to the large group of women like her who form a portion of society today.   Their lives are their own, they have few or no responsibilities and they are the envy of many women who are straining at the marriage yoke.   They are attractive to men, for they carry with them an air of sophistication and experience that is lacking in their compatriots, either married or single.   An either real or imaginary cleverness is attributed to them, while not infrequently they possess not a little cynicism.

"Bridgie" in *When Ladies Meet* is a combination of many characteristics.   She is shrewd, outspoken, cynical, and "an intelligent fool," as Mary Howard, her friend, calls her.   One is never quite sure just how much of her own conversation "Bridgie" really understands.   Is she being blunt and tactless unconsciously or is she aware of what she is saying?   When she says that she didn't feel nearly so bad when her husband died as she did when he was having an affair, we know she is speaking a fundamental truth for all women.   Do women like "Bridgie" rattle on incessantly because they see that they are being amusing and know that they can fool people under this guise, or are they unable to check their torrent of words?   It is a mystery that no man will ever solve but a woman might be able to tell him.   Whatever the case may be, the widow is an excellent stage character.

We shall consider now a character who appears in many plays in a more or less impersonal role. By impersonal is meant that this individual frequently serves to fill the position of the voice of society in general. His or her sentiments reflect the universal sentiments of society.

Bronson Howard's *Young Mrs. Winthrop* contains a character of this kind in the person of an elderly lawyer who reunites Douglas and Constance Winthrop after they have agreed to separate. He appeals to them not only on the grounds of sentiment but from the point of view that society will take if they separate. He shows them the social wrong they are committing by their decision. In many ways he is a forerunner of several other characters who appear more or less in this capacity.

Philip Phillimore, in Langdon Mitchell's *New York Idea,* is the epitome of the conservative, conventional gentleman whose ways are embedded in one groove only. Even though he is marrying a second time the event causes no ripple in his daily life. His aunt, Miss Heneage, is, if possible, even more correct. She has taken into her own hands the arrangements for the coming wedding, including the wording of the announcements. "The announcement Philip himself made was quite out of the question." Regarding the one she wrote she observes:

> "In my opinion it barely escapes sounding nasty. However, it is correct. The only remaining question is—to whom the announcement should not be sent. I consider the announcement of the wedding of two divorced persons to be in the nature of an intimate communication. It not only announces the wedding —it also announces the divorce." (She returns to her teacup.)

Her subsequent discussions as to whom she will send announcements and to whom she will not send them are among the most delightful bits in the play.

Probably Philip's most characteristic statement is when he tells Cynthia, his future wife, that it is "This hour of tea and toast and tranquility" that he values most in the whole day. The slightest sidestep from the path of decorum is to him, and so many like him, a major offense. He and his aunt, Miss Heneage, are immovable rocks upon which conventional society may forever depend.

In Jesse Lynch Williams' *Why Marry?* there is in the character of the Judge, Uncle Everett, a voice of society protesting against the unfortunate regulations concerning marriage and divorce. Helen and Jean are sisters. Jean's parents are forcing her into marriage with a man she does not love while Helen, having seen enough at home, refuses to marry the man she loves but announces that she will live with him. The Judge sees her side but shows how she cannot pursue this course. "She is the New Woman! Society can no longer force females into wedlock—so it is forcing them out—by the thousands! Approve of it? Of course not. But what good will our disapproval do? They will only laugh at you.—Unless society wakes up and reforms its rules and regulations of marriage, marriage is doomed." Later he says, "Marriage *is* in a bad way, but it's the less of two evils." Finally, by the authority vested in him as a judge by the state, Uncle Everett tricks Helen and Ernest Hamilton into marriage to save their self-respect in the eyes of the world, but he winds up with the warning "Yes, Respectability has triumphed this time, but let Society take warning and beware! beware! beware!"

In Williams' *Why Not?* which shows two married couples exchanging partners and all living happily together, we have a lawyer who tries to prevent them from doing this. He tells them that they have no grounds for divorce in their state unless they commit adultery, which is a grim commentary upon the divorce laws in this country. *Why Marry?* and *Why Not?* are two of the most penetrating studies we have in drama upon the questions of marriage and divorce and in each play Williams has created a character whose opinions may be called the voice of society.

We have noted Miss Heneage in *The New York Idea* displaying the feminine viewpoint of conservative society—strict adherence to every detail so that not the slightest trace of criticism can arise. When we come to Mrs. Boucicault, the dowager, in Rachel Crothers' *Let Us Be Gay* we confront a quite different woman.

Mrs. Boucicault abided by the rules of society in her day because she felt that she ought to be respectable but times have changed and she no longer pays much attention to codes and creeds. She thoroughly approves of divorce, is delighted to have seen her daughter get three, and is sorry that in her day it wasn't respectable for her to divorce her faithless husband. Mrs. Boucicault does as she pleases, accepts people for themselves, if they amuse her. She gathers around her groups of people she considers interesting and diverting and, provided they don't bother her, they are quite free to do as they please. She is a woman who has observed life very closely, who has pierced the bubble of hypocrisy, for she knows that all the laws in the world are not going to make angels out of human beings. She represents the changing standards of the feminine element in society.

These characters whom we have discussed are generally representative of the people whom one meets and knows. Some of them stand for the fundamental laws upon which society depends for its support while others reveal the forces which are in opposition to society. The characters in social comedy are interesting because they differ widely and because each one of them is a part of the life around us. From them we learn the viewpoint of the different generations, and the changing standards of both men and women. They are all very real people in whom we are interested because we come in contact with them constantly in our daily lives.

CHAPTER IV

CONCLUSION

When we survey American social comedy from Royall Tyler's *The Contrast* (1787), to S. N. Behrman's *End of Summer* (1936), we have an animated social history which deals not only with the various superficial aspects of society but which shows the fundamental changes of which social life is only one evidence. During each period of our history American playwrights have reflected contemporary manners, customs and problems. Royall Tyler revealed the strong patriotic spirit that gripped the new Republic as well as the social intrigues of that day. Mrs. Mowatt and Mrs. Bateman pictured the mid-nineteenth century rush for money and the new rich class that was rising. Bronson Howard studied the effects of the pressure of modern business upon society. He showed how the demands upon a man's time are so constant that his marriage may be ruined. William Dean Howells dealt, not only with an outside influence like business upon society, but purely with social life itself. At the turn of the century Clyde Fitch painted the picture of New York society and the struggles of individuals to maintain their positions. His sharp observations disclose to us the methods of social warfare and bring to light the superficial customs of his day. Langdon Mitchell and Jesse Lynch Williams dealt with the problems that the institutions of marriage and divorce present to society. Finally, James Forbes, Gilbert Emery, Rachel Crothers, Philip Barry and S. N. Behrman paint a panorama of post-war conditions in the social life of America. Here we see the revolt of the younger generation, the woman with a public career, the modern outlook upon marriage, and the introduction into the drawing room of discussions of contemporary political and national movements.

Through every period of American history there have been social comedies to reflect contemporary manners and thought. The development of the drama in this particular field has paralelled

143

the development of social life in this country. The many new problems which confront each age in American life are reflected by the playwrights of those respective ages.

Since women give the tone to society and their singleness of purpose, namely, to become happy "wives and mothers" which is evident from *The Contrast* to *End of Summer,* is their chief aim, the continuity of American social comedy is not so remarkable. The competitive instincts of women quite naturally have been more consistently devoted to personal distinction, either through love or marriage. Their pursuit of a career has been usually a disturbing element, but since in social comedy this pursuit is not so frequent, the competition of women has been more uniform than that of men. This has been more varied in America than in France or England, and the professional or business competition of men is also a disturbing element in social comedy. If we had a leisure class to the extent of that which exists in England or France we would have more male characters suited for social comedy. Since in nearly all plays there are more male characters than female, and since the male population of America is largely absorbed in business, the result has naturally been a more limited field for social comedy.

BIBLIOGRAPHY AND PLAY LIST

In this bibliography where place of publication or of performance is omitted, "New York" is to be understood.

ANSPACHER, LOUIS KAUFMAN
  The Unchastened Woman. 1916. (Thirty-ninth St. Theatre, Oct. 9, 1915)
BARKER, JAMES NELSON
  Tears and Smiles. Phila., 1808. (Chestnut, March 4, 1807)
BARRY, PHILIP
  You and I. 1925. (Belmont Theatre, Feb. 19, 1923)
  The Youngest. 1925. (Gaiety Theatre, Dec. 22, 1924)
  In a Garden. 1926. (Plymouth Theatre, Nov. 16, 1925)
  White Wings. 1927. (Booth Theatre, Oct. 15, 1926)
  Paris Bound. 1929. (Broad St. Theatre, Newark, Dec. 20, 1927, as *The Wedding.* Music Box Theatre, Dec. 27, 1927, as *Paris Bound*)
  Holiday. 1929. (Plymouth Theatre, Nov. 26, 1928)
  Hotel Universe. 1930. (Martin Beck Theatre, April 14, 1930)
BATEMAN, MRS. SIDNEY F.
  Self. N. Y. (1856) (Laura Keene's Theatre, N. Y., May 10, 1856)
  The Golden Calf: or, Marriage à la Mode. St. Louis, 1857. Wood's Theatre, St. Louis, August 31, 1857)
BEHRMAN, SAMUEL NATHANIEL
  The Second Man. 1927. Also in *Three Plays.* 1934. (Guild Theatre, April 11, 1927)
  Biography. 1933. (Guild Theatre, Dec. 12, 1932)
  Rain from Heaven. 1935. (John Golden Theatre, Dec. 24, 1934)
  End of Summer. 1936. (Bushnell Memorial Theatre, Hartford, Conn., Jan. 30, 1936; Guild Theatre, Feb. 17, 1936)
BELASCO, DAVID
  Lord Chumley. With Henry C. De Mille MS. (Lyceum Theatre, Aug. 21, 1888)
  The Charity Ball. With Henry C. De Mille MS. (Lyceum Theatre, Nov. 19, 1889)
BOKER, GEORGE HENRY
  The World a Mask. MS. dated 1851. (Walnut, April 21, 1851)
  The Widow's Marriage. In *Plays and Poems,* Boston, 1856.
BROUGHAM, JOHN
  The Musard Ball: or, Love at the Academy. N. Y. (1858). Burton's Theatre, 1857)

145

BROWN, IRVING
 Our Best Society. Adap. from Geo. Wm. Curtis' *Potiphar Papers.* 1876.
BUCHANAN, THOMPSON
 A Woman's Way. 1915. (Davidson Theatre, Milwaukee, Jan. 7, 1909;
 Hackett Theatre, Feb. 22, 1909)
BUNCE, OLIVER BELL
 Love in '76. N. Y. (1857) (Laura Keene's Theatre, N. Y., Feb. 28,
 1857)
CROTHERS, RACHEL
 Nice People. In Quinn's *Contemporary American Plays.* (Atlantic
 City, N. J., Dec. 26, 1920; Klaw Theatre, March 2, 1921)
 Mary the Third. 1923. (Thirty-ninth St. Theatre, Feb. 5, 1923)
 Expressing Willie. 1924. (Forty-eighth St. Theatre, April 16, 1924)
 Let Us Be Gay. 1929. (Little Theatre, Feb. 21, 1929)
 As Husbands Go. 1931. (John Golden Theatre, March 5, 1931)
 When Ladies Meet. 1932. (Royal Theatre, Oct. 6, 1932)
DALY, AUGUSTIN
 Divorce. Priv. printed, 1884. (Fifth Ave. Theatre, Sept. 5, 1871; Thea-
 tre Royal, Edinburgh, Dec. 12, 1881)
 Pique. Priv. printed, 1884. (New Fifth Ave. Theatre, Dec. 14, 1875;
 as *Only a Woman,* Brighton Theatre Royal, Oct. 16, 1882; as *Her
 Own Enemy,* Gaiety Theatre, London, March 26, 1884)
 Lemons. Adap. of *Citronen* by Julius Rosen. Priv. printed 1877. (New
 Fifth Ave. Theatre, Jan. 15, 1875)
 The Passing Regiment. Adap. of *Krieg im Frieden* by G. von Moser
 and F. von Schönthan. Priv. printed, 1884. (Daly's Theatre,
 Nov. 10, 1881)
 Our English Friend. Adap. of *Reif von Reiflingen* by G. von Moser.
 Priv. printed, 1884. (Daly's Theatre, Nov. 25, 1882)
 Love on Crutches. Adap. of *Ihre Ideale* by Heinrich Stopitzer. Priv.
 printed, 1884. (Daly's Theatre, Nov. 25, 1884)
 Love in Harness. Adap. of *Bonheur Conjugal* by Albin Valabrégue.
 Priv. printed, 1887. (Daly's Theatre, Nov. 16, 1886)
 The Railroad of Love. Adap. of *Goldfische* by F. von Schönthan and
 G. Kadelburg. Priv. printed, 1887. (Daly's Theatre, Nov. 1,
 1887)
 The Lottery of Love. Adap. of *Les Suprises du Divorce* by Alexandre
 Bisson and Antony Mars. Priv. printed 1889. (Daly's Theatre
 Oct. 9, 1888)
 The Last Word. Adap. of *Das Letzte Wort* by F. von Schönthan.
 Priv. printed, 1891. (Daly's Theatre, Oct. 28, 1890)
 Love in Tandem. Adap. of *Vie à Deux* by Henri Bocage and Charles
 de Courcy. Priv. printed. (Daly's Theatre, Feb. 9, 1892)
 The Countess Gucki. From German of F. von Schönthan. Priv.
 printed, 1895. (Daly's Theatre, Jan. 28, 1896)

DE MILLE, HENRY C.
John Delmar's Daughters. Priv. printed, C.1883. (Madison Square
Theatre, Dec. 10, 1883)
DODD, LEE WILSON
The Changelings. 1924 (Henry Miller Theatre, Sept. 17, 1923)
DUNLAP, WILLIAM
The Father: or, American Shandy-ism. N. Y. 1789. (John St.
Theatre, Sept. 7, 1789)
EMERY, GILBERT
Episode. (MS. Univ. of Penna.) (Bijou Theatre, Feb. 4, 1925)
Love-in-a-Mist. With Amelie Rives (Princess Troubetzkoy) c. 1926.
(Gaiety Theatre, April 12, 1926)
FAWCETT, EDGAR
The Buntling Ball. 1884
FITCH, CLYDE
Beau Brummell. 1908. (Madison Square Theatre, May 17, 1890)
A Modern Match. MS. (Union Square Theatre, March 14, 1892;
Royalty Theatre, London, as *Marriage* 1892, Oct. 28, 1892)
His Grace de Grammont. MS. (Rockford, Ill., Sept 22, 1894.
Grand Opera House, Chicago, Sept. 24, 1894)
Barbara Frietchie. 1900. (Broad St. Theatre, Phila., Oct. 10, 1899;
Criterion Theatre, Oct. 23, 1899)
The Climbers. 1906. (Bijou Theatre, Jan. 15, 1901; Comedy Theatre,
London, Sept. 5, 1903)
The Stubbornness of Geraldine. 1906. (Garrick Theatre, Nov. 3, 1902)
The Girl with the Green Eyes. 1905. (Savoy Theatre, Dec. 25, 1902)
Her Own Way. 1907. (Star Theatre, Buffalo, Sept. 24, 1903; Gar-
rick Theatre, Sept. 28, 1903; Lyric Theatre, London, April 25,
1905)
Her Great Match. In Quinn's *Representative American Plays.* Early
Editions. (Syracuse, Sept. 1, 1905; Criterion Theatre, Sept. 4,
1905)
The Truth. 1907. (Cleveland, Ohio, Oct. 15, 1906; Criterion Theatre,
Jan. 7, 1907; Comedy Theatre, London, April 6, 1907; Neues
Theatre, Berlin, Sept. 24, 1908; Little Theatre, April 14, 1914)
FLEXNER, ANNE CRAWFORD
The Marriage Game. 1916. (Comedy Theatre, Oct. 29, 1913)
FORBES, JAMES
The Famous Mrs. Fair. c.1920. (Academy, Baltimore, Dec. 15, 1919;
Henry Miller Theatre, Dec. 22, 1919)
GOODRICH, ARTHUR
So This is London! c.1926. (Hudson Theatre, Aug. 30, 1922)
HOWARD, BRONSON
Saratoga: or, Pistols for Seven. c.1870. (Fifth Ave. Theatre, Dec.
21, 1870; Court Theatre, London, as *Brighton*, May 25, 1874)

Old Love Letters. Priv. printed, 1897. (Park Theatre, Aug. 31, 1878)
Young Mrs. Winthrop. c.1899. (Madison Square Theatre, Oct. 9, 1882; Marylebone Theatre, London, Sept. 21, 1882 (copyright); Court Theatre, London, Nov. 6, 1884)
One of Our Girls. Priv. printed, 1897. (Lyceum Theatre, Nov. 10, 1885)
The Henrietta. Priv. printed, 1901. (Union Square Theatre, Sept. 26, 1887; Knickerbocker Theatre, Dec. 22, 1913, as *The New Henrietta*)
Aristocracy. Priv. printed, 1898. (Palmer's Theatre, Nov. 14, 1892)
Kate. 1906.

HOWELLS, WILLIAM DEAN
 A Counterfeit Presentment. Boston, c.1877. (Grand Opera House, Cincinnati, O., Oct. 11, 1877)
 The Sleeping Car. Boston, 1883.
 The Register. Boston, 1884.
 The Elevator. Boston, 1885.
 Five O'clock Tea. c.1889.
 The Mouse Trap. c.1889.
 A Likely Story. c.1889.
 A Letter of Introduction. 1892.
 The Unexpected Guests. 1893.
 Evening Dress. 1893.
 An Indian Giver. 1900.

HURLBURT, WILLIAM HENRY
 Americans in Paris: or, A Game of Dominoes. N. Y. (1858). (Wallack's Theatre, N. Y., May 8, 1858)

HUTTON, JOSEPH
 Fashionable Follies. Phila. 1815.

KUMMER, CLARE
 Good Gracious, Annabelle. c.1922. (Republic Theatre, Oct. 31, 1916)
 Rollo's Wild Oat. c.1922. (Columbia Theatre, Far Rockaway, N. Y., Jan. 30, 1920; Punch and Judy Theatre, Nov. 23, 1920)

LOW, SAMUEL
 The Politician Outwitted. N. Y. 1789.

MACKAYE, PERCY
 Anti-Matrimony. 1910. (Garrick Theatre, N. Y., Sept. 22, 1910)

MATTHEWS, BRANDER
 This Picture and That. 1894. (Lyceum Theatre, April 15, 1887)
 The Decision of the Court. 1893. (Hermann's Theatre, March 23, 1893)

MITCHELL, LANGDON ELWYN
 The New York Idea. Boston, 1908. (Lyric Theatre, Nov. 19, 1906; Kammerspiel Theatre, Berlin, Oct. 7, 1916)

MOWATT, ANNA C. O. (RITCHIE)
> *Fashion: or, Life in New York.* London, 1850. (Park, March 24, 1845)

PAYNE, JOHN HOWARD
> *Charles the Second: or, The Merry Monarch.* With Washington Irving. London, 1824. (Covent Garden, London, May 27, 1824; Park, Oct. 25, 1824)

TARKINGTON, NEWTON BOOTH
> *Tweedles.* With H. L. Wilson. 1924. (Frazee Theatre, Aug. 13, 1923)

THOMAS, ALBERT ELLSWORTH
> *Her Husband's Wife.* 1914. (Broad St. Theatre, Phila., Feb. 14, 1910; Garrick Theatre, April 9, 1910; New Theatre, London, Sept. 15, 1916)
> *The Rainbow.* c.1919. (Liberty Theatre, March 11, 1912)
> *The Better Understanding.* With Clayton Hamilton. Boston, 1924. (Columbia Theatre, San Francisco, May, 1917)
> *Just Suppose.* c.1923. (Academy, Baltimore, Md., May 17, 1920; Henry Miller Theatre, Nov. 1, 1920)
> *No More Ladies.* 1933. (Chestnut St. Opera House, Phila., Dec. 23, 1933; Booth Theatre, Jan. 23, 1934)

THOMAS, AUGUSTUS
> *The Other Girl.* c.1917. (Criterion Theatre, Dec. 29. 1903)
> *Mrs. Leffingwell's Boots.* c.1916. (Savoy Theatre, Jan. 11, 1905)
> *The Earl of Pawtucket.* c.1917. (Madison Square Theatre, Feb. 5, 1903; Playhouse, London, June 25, 1907)

TYLER, ROYALL
> *The Contrast.* Phila., 1790. (John St. Theatre, April 16, 1787)

WAINWRIGHT, D. W.
> *Wheat and Chaff.* N. Y. (1858). (Wallack's Theatre, N. Y., Oct. 30, 1858)

WILKINS, E. G. P.
> *My Wife's Mirror.* N. Y. (1856) (Laura Keene's Theatre, N. Y., May 10, 1856)
> *Young New York.* N. Y. n. d. (Laura Keene's Theatre, N. Y., Nov. 24, 1856)

WILLIAMS, JESSE LYNCH
> *Why Marry?* Published as *And So They Were Married.* 1914. Revised as acting version of *Why Marry?* In Quinn's *Contemporary American Plays.* (Columbus, O., Nov. 1, 1917; Astor Theatre, Dec. 25, 1917)
> *Why Not?* Dram. of novelette by author, *Remating Time.* Boston, 1924. (Forty-eighth St. Theatre, Dec. 25, 1922)

ANONYMOUS
> *Sans Souci, alias Free and Easy: or, An Evening's Peep into a Polite Circle.* Boston, 1785.

GENERAL BACKGROUND

ALLEN, FREDERICK LEWIS:
Only Yesterday, 1931.
BEARD, CHARLES AND MARY:
The Rise of American Civilization, 1930.
BRADLEY, A. G.:
Colonial Americans in Exile, 1932.
BREMER, FREDERIKA
The Homes of the New World. Impressions of America, Vol. II, 1858.
CLARK, BARRETT H.:
The British and American Drama of Today, 1915.
A Study of the Modern Drama, 1925.
An Hour of American Drama, 1930.
COAD, ORAL S. AND MIMS, EDWIN, JR.:
The American Stage, Vol. XIV of *The Pageant of America,* 1929.
DALY, JOSEPH FRANCIS:
The Life of Augustin Daly, 1917.
DICKINSON, THOMAS H.:
Playwrights of the New American Theatre, 1925.
DUNLAP, WILLIAM:
History of the American Theatre, 1832.
EATON, WALTER PRITCHARD:
"At the New Theatre and Others." (*The American Stage: Its Problems and Performances,* 1908-1910), 1910.
GRANT, ANN L.:
Memoirs of an American Lady, (1846).
HAMILTON, CLAYTON:
Problems of the Playwright, 1917.
HORNBLOW, ARTHUR:
A History of the Theatre in America from Its Beginning to the Present Time, 2 Vols., Phila., 1919.
HUTTON, LAURENCE:
Curiosities of the American Stage, 1891.
MADEIRA, LOUIS C.:
Music in Philadelphia and the Musical Fund Society, 1896.
MATTHEWS, BRANDER:
The Development of the Drama, 1904.
A Study of the Drama, 1910.
MOSES, MONTROSE J.:
The American Dramatist, 1911. Rev. 1925.
The American Theatre as Seen by Its Critics. Edited by Montrose J. Moses and John Mason Brown, 1934.
MUZZEY, DAVID SAVILLE:
An American History, 1923.

PARRINGTON, VERNON LOUIS:
Main Currents in American Thought, 4 Vol., 1927.

PEACOCK, VIRGINIA TATNALL:
Famous American Belles of the Nineteenth Century, 1901.

PHELPS, WILLIAM LYON:
Essay on Modern Dramatists, 1921.

THE ARISTOCRATIC JOURNEY:
Being the Outspoken Letters of Mrs. Basil Hall Written during a Fourteen Months' Sojourn in America, 1827-28. Prefaced and edited by Una Pope-Hennessy, 1931.

QUINN, ARTHUR HOBSON:
A History of the American Drama from the Beginning to the Civil War, 1923.
A History of the American Drama from the Civil War to the Present Day, 2 Vol., 1927. Rev. 1936 in one volume.

REED, ISAAC PERLEY:
Realistic Presentation of American Characters in Native American Plays Prior to 1870. Pub. by Univ. at Columbus, Ohio, 1894.

SCHOENBERGER, HAROLD WILLIAM:
American Adaptations of French Plays on the New York and Philadelphia Stages from 1790 to 1833, 1924.

SONNECK, O. G.:
Early Concert Life in America, 1907.
Early Opera in America, 1915.

SULLIVAN, MARK:
Our Times, 1926.

WARE, RALPH HARTMAN:
American Adaptations of French Plays on the New York and Philadelphia Stages from 1834 to the Civil War, 1930.

WHARTON, ANNE HOLLINGSWORTH:
Social Life in The Early Republic, 1902.
Colonial Days and Dames, 1900.